# Lions

by Vince Melocchi

A SAMUEL FRENCH ACTING EDITION

SAMUEL FRENCH
FOUNDED 1830

NEW YORK HOLLYWOOD LONDON TORONTO

SAMUELFRENCH.COM

## MUSIC NOTE

## IMPORTANT BILLING AND CREDIT REQUIREMENTS

Pacific Resident Theatre presents

# LIONS

by
## VINCE MELOCCHI

Directed by
## GUILLERMO CIENFUEGOS

Produced by
## LISA NICHOLS

Stage Manager
## SHRUTI KRISHNAN

Set and Sound Design
## GUILLERMO CIENFUEGOS

Lighting Design
## WILLIAM WILDAY

Costume Coordinator
## SARAH ZINSSER

Video Design
## KEITH STEVENSON

Prop Master/Set Dressing
## DAN COLE

Set Construction
## NORMAN SCOTT

*LIONS* premiered on October 24, 2008 at the Pacific Resident Theatre, Venice, CA; Marilyn Fox, Artistic Director. The production was directed by Guillermo Cienfuegos and produced by Lisa Nichols with the following cast:

JOHN "SPOOK" WAITE . . . . . . . . . . . . . . . . . . . . . . . . . . . Matt McKenzie
LEON "BISCUIT" CROISSANT . . . . . . . . . . . . . . Haskell V. Anderson III
ANDY GUERALL . . . . . . . . . . . . . . . . . . . . . . . . . . . . . . . Keith Stevenson
BILL "HOUSEPIE" FOLINO . . . . . . . . . . . . . . . . . . . . . . . . . . . Dan Cole
CURTIS SAWYER . . . . . . . . . . . . . . . . . . . . . . . . . . . . . Malik B. El-Amin
BETH WAITE . . . . . . . . . . . . . . . . . . . . . . . . . . . . . . . . Valerie Dillman
ARTIE PIRO . . . . . . . . . . . . . . . . . . . . . . . . . . . . . . . . . . . Nick Rogers
GAIL FINCH . . . . . . . . . . . . . . . . . . . . . . . . . . . . . . . . . Sarah Zinsser
LARRY GERBER . . . . . . . . . . . . . . . . . . . . . . . . . . . . . Seth Margolies
REVEREND RUSSELL STUYVANTS . . . . . . . . . . . . . . . . . . . . Kim Estes
MABEL JOHNSON . . . . . . . . . . . . . . . . . . . . . . . . . . . . Gloria Charles
JERRY "LENNIE" LENHART . . . . . . . . . . . . . . . . . . . Ron E. Dickinson
CHICAGO GUY, THAT'S RIGHT . . . . . . . . . . . . . . . . . . . Dan Kozlowski
VOICE ACTORS . . . . . . . . . . . . . . . . . . . . Melody Doyle, Terrance Elton,
Mark Henry, Justin Levine, Alex Fernandez

UNDERSTUDIES/REPLACEMENTS

Alan Keith Caldwell
Scott Conte
Christopher L. Davis
Terrance Elton
Alex Fernandez
Shon Fuller
Marty Lodge
Clarinda Ross
Will Rothaar
Stan Sellers

# CHARACTERS

**JOHN "SPOOK" WAITE** – Late forties, an unemployed factory worker.

**LEON "BISCUIT" CROISSANT** – African-American. Late forties, works for the Detroit morgue.

**ANDY GUERALL** – Early thirties. Bartender at The 10th Ward Club.

**BILL "HOUSEPIE" FOLINO** – Late fifties.

**CURTIS SAWER** – African American. Late twenties. Grocery store bagger.

**BETH WAITE** – John's wife. Mid forties.

**ARTIE PIRO** – Twenty-four, childhood friend of John Waite. Appears only in memory.

**GAIL FINCH** – Mid forties. Waitress at the local diner.

**LARRY GERBER** – Late forties, local pizza shop owner.

**REVEREND RUSSELL STUVANTS** – African American. Early fifties, a man of the cloth.

**MABEL JOHNSON** – African American. Late-fifties. A job placement counselor.

**JERRY "LENNIE" LENHART** – Bartender at The 10th ward club.

**MAN** (aka **CHICAGO**) – A Chicago Bears fan.

**NOTE:** The same actor can play both Chicago and Lennie.

## TIME

April 2007 through February 2008.

## PLACE

West Detroit, Michigan

## AUTHOR'S NOTE

The play takes place during the 2007-2008 National Football League season (Draft Day, April, 2007 through the Super Bowl February 2008). In the original production, the passage of time was indicated by the use of audio clips, as well as video projections of football games and the running tally of the Lions record. These elements helped to frame the chronology of the season.

I would encourage future producers to explore and employ audio clips as they see fit for their own productions, with the understanding that those producers are responsible for obtaining rights to any clips ultimately used in performance.

# The 10th Ward Club – Draft Day, April 2007

*(THE 10TH WARD CLUB.)*

*(The club is very old school. A small horseshoe bar fills the upstage left area.)*

*(On the wall next to the bar, letters spell out, "The 10th Ward Club." Below the lettering is a plaque with the names of members, past and present.)*

*(A pool table rests upstage right. On the wall next to it, hangs an old mirror, peppered with bumpers stickers. A dartboard, with a picture of the Detroit Lions general manager, Matt Millen tacked over it, hangs on the downstage wall. Across the room, a small coffee table and assorted chairs fill the downstage left area. The wood panelled walls are covered with sports pennants from the local teams as well as pictures of Detroit sports heroes and club members.)*

*(An imaginary television set hangs downstage, above the audience. This is the set the actors will refer to during the action.)*

*(As the lights rise, the audio portion from the 2007 NFL Draft is heard. The members of the club are downstage staring at the TV.)*

*(Pacing nervously is* **JOHN "SPOOK" WAITE**, *late forties, blue collar. Although still strong and in good shape, he has a heaviness about him. He wears a Detroit Lions T-shirt and blue jeans. He will be wearing this attire through the entire play, except where noted.)*

**ANNOUNCER.** *(V.O.)*...with the first pick in the 2007 NFL Draft, the Oakland Raiders select...quarterback JaMarcus Russell from Louisiana State University. The Detroit Lions are now on the clock...

**SPOOK.** Yes! Alright, here we go…we're on the clock! True to form, Oakland goes with Russell.

*(**LARRY GERBER**, a good natured man in his late 40s, and owner of the pizza shop next door chimes in. He wears a Detroit Lions football jersey.)*

**LARRY.** That means we get Johnson!

*(**SPOOK** crosses to the dartboard, faces the Matt Millen picture stuck to it.)*

**SPOOK.** *(to photo)* Don't fuck this up. Do not fuck this up.

*(Sitting at the bar, laughing at **SPOOK**'s agitation and concern, is **GAIL FINCH**. A diminutive, plain woman in her mid-40s. She is dressed in Green Bay Packers attire.)*

**SPOOK.** I know you want to fuck this up. But don't. Fifteen minutes before we get Johnson.

**GAIL.** Tick, tock.

**SPOOK.** Fifteen minutes for you to screw it up completely.

*(Sitting in a chair behind **SPOOK** is **REVEREND STU-VANTS**. An African-American man in his early 50s. Handsome and with a terrific amount of charm, he is the voice of reason in the club.)*

**REV.** He'll be fine. Matt Millen will make the right decision. *(**SPOOK** nods, sits in a chair resting center stage. Note: While in the club, he will always sit in this chair unless specifically noted.)*

**GAIL.** Hey Larry, it's Saturday. Why aren't you at the shop?

**LARRY.** Ownership has it's privileges. So the Raiders took JaMarcus Russell!

**REV.** Al Davis loves that vertical game.

**LARRY.** *(to SPOOK)* What do you think?

**GAIL.** Think you should've brought over a couple of pizzas from next door.

**LARRY.** Sure. Always lookin' for a handout, ya big mooch.

**GAIL.** Remember that the next time you come over to Shorty's askin' for extra slaw.

**LARRY.** Think he's worth the number one pick?

**SPOOK.** (Has a) Cannon of an arm, feel for the big play, great leader, but suspect work ethic. Thing to worry about though, is that wrist that kept him out of the Peach Bowl in '05. Good Rose Bowl, but who'd L.S.U. play – Besides, we're talkin' about the Raiders, so who gives two shits, right?

**LARRY.** Guy is set for life.

**SPOOK.** Bum wrist or no, yeah.

**LARRY.** Speakin' of set for life, I see Artie Piro represents a couple of these guys today.

(**ANDY GUERALL,** *the bartender, has been talking on the phone behind the bar. Finishing his conversation, he crosses downstage. In his early 30s, he has a quick wit and a thirst for knowledge.*)

**ANDY.** Housepie says "Hi."

**LARRY.** He's there already?

**ANDY.** Yep.

**GAIL.** So he really went?

**ANDY.** Yesterday.

**LARRY.** Can't believe it.

**SPOOK.** Wouldn't ya love to see his face if Sarge found out?

**GAIL.** Kill him.

**LARRY.** *Pay* to see that. What he tell her?

**ANDY.** Had to fly to Colorado for medical reasons.

**GAIL.** And they met, how?

**ANDY.** Phone. She handles his AARP reimbursement claims.

**GAIL.** If my husband pulled that crap –

**LARRY.** What husband?

**GAIL.** Sayin'...*if* my husband...

**LARRY.** And I'm sayin', what husband?

**GAIL.** And I'm sayin' fuck off.

(*The phone rings.*)

**SPOOK.** *(to* **ANDY***)* I ain't here.

(**ANDY** *answers it.*)

**SPOOK.** Larry, may as well have one.

**LARRY.** Yeah, got Lefty next door.

(**ANDY** *hangs up.*)

**ANDY.** Spook, that was Beth.

**SPOOK.** Thank you.

**GAIL.** Honestly, how can Sarge let him go out there?

**SPOOK.** Thinks it's medical, right?

**ANDY.** Well, it *is* medical, y'know what I mean?

**GAIL.** S*een* her?

**ANDY.** Yeah. Saw a picture a couple days ago.

**GAIL.** And…?

**ANDY.** She looks like a man.

**GAIL.** C'mon!

**ANDY.** Got them summer teeth. Some are here, some are there.

**LARRY.** So he's flyin' out there for a taste from a woman he ain't even met?

**ANDY.** Talked on the phone a lot.

**LARRY.** And she looks like a man? Uh.

**ANDY.** Look what she's gettin', okay?

**GAIL.** What's her name?

**ANDY.** Roberta somethin'. All I know is she works for AARP, lives in Colorado and looks like a man.

**SPOOK.** Fuckin' Housepie.

**GAIL.** Colorado, huh? Wonder if I can get somebody to fly out here and fuck me. *(They all look at her. beat)* Where's he stayin'?

**ANDY.** Guess with that lady Roberta.

**LARRY.** "Colorado Bob"!

**ANDY.** You're brutal.

**LARRY.** *You* said she looks like a man. Anyway, he ain't here.

**ANDY.** Can you imagine that scene out there?

**LARRY.** Love to have "Bill-Cam," huh?

**ANDY.** By the way, you never heard about "Colorado Bob." Far as you guys know, he's visiting "his cousin."

**REV.** It's a lonely man that walks in the shadow of deceit.

**ANDY.** Why he's with Colorado Bob, Rev. He's lonely.

**REV.** He's married and living a lie.

**LARRY.** Draft Day, Rev –

**REV.** Walking hand in hand with Satan himself –

**LARRY.** Draft day!

*(Behind the bar, a buzzer sounds. ANDY presses a button located next to the register. Throughout the play, this same action will precede most entrances made from the outside.)*

**ANDY.** 10th Ward Club.

**BISCUIT.** *(O.S.)* Biscuit.

**LARRY.** Finally!

*(SPOOK runs upstage, jumps on a chair by the side of the doorway. He motions to the rest of the members to remain quiet.)*

*(LEON "BISCUIT" CROISSANT hustles in. Early 50s, African-American, he is lean and wiry, and dressed in his work attire, which resembles a haz mat suit. As he passes by, SPOOK pounces on top of him.)*

**SPOOK.** What the shit, Biscuit? Where you been?

*(SPOOK and BISCUIT throw soft jabs at each other.)*

**BISCUIT.** Paged.

**SPOOK.** Draft day?

**BISCUIT.** Got to work, brother. Death don't care 'bout no draft. Had to bag an old man over John R. Sittin' on a bench. Starin'. Mouth open. Just like he was frozen an' shit.

**REV.** Lord have mercy on his soul.

**BISCUIT.** Everybody got to go sometime. What's happenin', Rev? Pizza King?

*(BISCUIT crosses upstage. Sits.)*

**BISCUIT.** Russell go first?

**SPOOK.** Yeah.

**BISCUIT.** One rich young brother.

*(A **MAN** walks in unannounced. He wears a Chicago Bears jersey.)*

**ANDY.** I help you?

**MAN.** Yeah. Stroh's.

**ANDY.** How'd you get in here?

**MAN.** Walked in.

**ANDY.** Biscuit?

**BISCUIT.** Must of left it open. My bad.

**ANDY.** Guys gotta watch that shit. *(to **MAN**)* Sorry, buddy. This is a private club. Gotta be a member, so –

**MAN.** Huh. Still get a drink?

**SPOOK.** Wearin' a Bears jersey? You wanna sit in a club with a bunch of Lions fans and watch the draft?

**MAN.** Yeah.

**LARRY.** Give him credit. He's got balls.

**MAN.** Guys, I just wanna grab a brew, an' see who we get.

**ANDY.** Need to be a member.

**MAN.** For a neighborhood bar?

**ANDY.** Like I said, this ain't a bar. It's a club. The 10th Ward Club. Gotta be a member, be sponsored, pay annual dues, all of that.

**MAN.** Another place I can go?

**LARRY.** Not around here. 'Member how this place used to be? Th' fuck happened?

**SPOOK.** It'll come back. Shit's cyclical.

**ANDY.** Anyway, look –

**MAN.** – Alright!. *(beat)* You guys pick yet?

**SPOOK.** Next.

**MAN.** Good luck. You take the kid from Georgia Tech you might finally start winnin' a few.

**SPOOK.** What's that mean?

**MAN.** Sayin' Jon Kitna will have someone to throw to.

*(He starts to go.)*

**SPOOK.** Hold up. Grossman or Griese?

MAN. If we don't get offensive line help it won't matter.

SPOOK. Yep.

(MAN *starts to go again.*)

SPOOK. Hey, wait.

(SPOOK *approaches the others.*)

SPOOK. Let him stay for a beer.

ANDY. Can't! Against the by-laws of the club!

SPOOK. One beer. Jeez. I'll sponsor him.

ANDY. Gonna pay his guest fee, too?

(SPOOK *again appeals to the crowd.*)

SPOOK. C'mon, guys…

(*After a few moments, general agreement.*)

GAIL. Let him have a drink.

BISCUIT. Yeah. Let the dude hang.

ANDY. Nah, nah. There's risk management issues.

BISCUIT. Risk, what?

ANDY. Insurance. He falls or somethin', he can sue.

BISCUIT. You fall, you gonna sue?

MAN. My ass is onna fuckin' stool all day, makes this guy happy.

BISCUIT. See that. (*beat*) John, sponsor him. Shit, I'll sponsor the motherfucker.

ANDY. Have to do paperwork an' 'at…

BISCUIT. Take that pole out your ass, man.

SPOOK. Look, I've been a member for over twenty years, and –

MAN. You know what? Fuck this –

SPOOK. – shut up, Chicago. I've been a member for over twenty years, and if I wanna have a guest, I think I'm entitled. So, fuck you, Andy. (*to* MAN) Chicago, need five bucks for the guest fee.

(CHICAGO *hands him the money.*)

SPOOK. Here's the fee, give him a drink, alright!?

(ANDY *gives in and goes back behind the bar.*)

**ANDY.** Need to sign in. I.D, too.

**BISCUIT.** Hey Andy. Feel good, huh?

**ANDY.** What?

**BISCUIT.** Get that pole out your ass.

*(general laughter)*

**SPOOK.** Hey, Chicago. Favorite Bear?

**MAN.** Mike Phipps. *(off their reaction)* I was a kid, y'know?

*(groans)*

**REV.** Like an N.F.C North convention here. All we need is a Minnesota Vikings fan.

*(The man crosses downstage to sit. SPOOK waves him over to join the group. As he settles in, he notices everyone staring at him. SPOOK leans in.)*

**SPOOK.** Know, I hate the fuckin' Bears.

**MAN.** *(tense beat)* I hate the fuckin' Lions.

**SPOOK.** Way it should be.

*(They fist bump.)*

**ANDY.** Chicago guy got this round.

*(Cheers.)*

**SPOOK.** By the way, I'm Spook. You met Biscuit. That's Gail, the Cheesehead. This is Reverend Stuvants, keeps all us hillrats in line. Over there, that's Larry the Pizza King, best pie in the West Detroit area. And you met Andy, the man with the recently relaxed sphincter.

**MAN.** Appreciate this. Dyin' over that old bat's house.

**SPOOK.** Gotta watch the draft, right? *(beat)* What you do in the Windy City for work an' 'at?

**MAN.** Install carpet with Sullivan and Son. Good to get away, been workin' my balls off non stop. Fifty, sixty hour weeks.

**SPOOK.** Yeah, that's…

**MAN.** What do you do?

**SPOOK.** What I did.

**MAN.** Huh?

**SPOOK.** Did. Worked over Elias Metal, making screws and fasteners 'till they ran off to Mexico.

**MAN.** Sucks.

**SPOOK.** Yeah, pretty much. But somethin' else will come up. Besides, we still the got the Lions!

*(All cheer.)*

**LARRY.** Matt Millen better take Calvin Johnson.

**GAIL.** Another receiver? You guys ever gonna get it right?

**BISCUIT.** Please. How long we got to hear your mess?

**GAIL.** Fifteen more picks.

**LARRY.** Goddamn Packer fan. Why you even here?

**GAIL.** Cheap booze, jackass. Besides. I'm a member, remember?

**SPOOK.** Go back to Green Bay, will ya?

**GAIL.** You mean, "Titletown"?

*(a chorus of "boo's")*

**SPOOK.** Long time ago.

**BISCUIT.** I hear that.

**GAIL.** 1996. When's the last time the Lions won a title? Oh, that's right, never. One of six teams...

**LARRY.** Enough...

**SPOOK.** Different this year.

**GAIL.** Every year it's different.

**SPOOK.** Tellin' you, it is.

**GAIL.** Why? Give me one reason why this year –

**SPOOK.** Right here! This is why. Here we go!

*(pointing the remote)*

**ANNOUNCER** *(V.O.)* ...with the second pick in the 2007 NFL Draft the Detroit Lions select wide receiver Calvin Johnson from Georgia Tech University.

*(The place erupts with cheers, hugs, high fives, etc.)*

**SPOOK.** This year is different, 'cause this year...WE GOT CALVIN JOHNSON!!!!!

REV. Thank you, Lord! You have sent this righteous, young
       brother from the south to heal this city and it's fans!
       God bless the Detroit Lions!

    (**LARRY** *and* **BISCUIT** *begin singing the Lions fight
    song.* * *Eventually,* **REV** *and* **SPOOK** *join in.*)

    *(BLACKOUT)*

## 10th Ward Club – Preseason – August

(BISCUIT *sits center stage,* ANDY *is behind the bar.* BILL
"HOUSEPIE" FOLINO, *a heavyset man in his late 50s,
sits on his stool at the bar, drinking a beer. They watch
the TV.*)

TV ANNOUNCER. *(V.O.)* "...and this type of suicide is something we are seeing more and more of in Detroit and
surrounding areas. Why, authorities are not certain.
This is Susan Walker reporting..."

(BISCUIT *hits the mute button on the remote.*)

BISCUIT. Suicide, homicide, whatever side. They go, you
call me. Shit...

ANDY. Don't know how you do it, Biscuit.

BISCUIT. Hunger make folks do some strange shit. How old
was you when Elias left?

ANDY. Ah, about twenty-nine.

BISCUIT. Alright. 'Steada bein' twenty fuckin' nine an' shit,
now you forty somethin'. Wife. Kids. Crib. Water, elec-
tric, an' shit. Autos ain't hirin' no more. Got no other
skills 'cept what you be doin' alla this time. An' you
too old to start over again. So what you gonna do?

ANDY. Hindsight? Them leavin' was the best thing happened
to me. Sleep walkin' since I got out of Thomas Jefferson.
Goin' back to school now. Plant was bullshit anyway.

BISCUIT. Ain't got no family. No ties.

ANDY. Not yet. Get done, get a job using my brain. Lots of
opportunities out there.

BISCUIT. For a single, white man.

ANDY. Here we go. Make your breaks.

BISCUIT. Boy, what world you livin' in?

ANDY. Got this Professor. Simonetta. He says, and I agree,
societal problems stem from class, not race. This time
next year, that guy from Illinois could be President.
Now he's black. Bet he faced a ton of adversity –

BISCUIT. First off, first off! Ain't no way this here redneck
country gonna elect a motherfuckin' black man.

ANDY. You don't think so?

BISCUIT. Hell, no. White folk say they goin' be votin' for the brother. Yeah, that's what they be sayin'. But once that curtain be closed, all they see is white, white, white.

ANDY. Your way of thinking is prehistoric.

*(The buzzer rings.)*

BISCUIT. You a bartender. Bar-tend.

(**REV** *enters from the rest room.*)

ANDY. Why don't you clean the cobwebs outta your head! It's guys like you that perpetuate that bullshit. When you gonna give that up.

(**ANDY** *answers the buzzer.*)

ANDY. 10th Ward.

CURTIS. *(O.S.)* Curtis.

ANDY. People aren't as narrow minded as you think.

BISCUIT. Fuck you know? Towns like Grosse Pointe, Bloomfield an' shit. I sees the looks on them folks faces when I walks in an' shit, "Oh, no. Here come the Negro."

(**CURTIS BENTON**, *an African-American man in his late twenties, enters.*)

CURTIS. Whats up everybody?

BISCUIT. What's up, Curtis?

REV. Grosse Pointe.

BISCUIT. What?

(**REV** *crosses to the bar.*)

REV. Andy, can I settle up?

ANDY. Sure.

REV. I couldn't of been more than nine or ten when my father took me to Grosse Pointe to hear Dr. Martin Luther King speak.

BILL. I remember that.

REV. Yeah, the speech was called the "The Other America." Powerful.

BILL. Big deal back then.

**REV.** Still is.

**BILL.** First time I ever saw a colored in Grosse Pointe.

(**REV, BISCUIT** and **CURTIS** *give him a surprised look.*
**BILL** *doesn't notice*)

**REV.** And the last, too. *(beat)* Biscuit. Andy. Shake hands.

**BISCUIT.** Say what?

**REV.** You heard me. Shake hands.

*(They reluctantly do so.)*

**REV.** Remember, it's all about respectin' each other. 'Night,
my brothers. Be well.

*(Goodbyes are said.)*

**BISCUIT.** Alright, Rev.

(**BISCUIT** *makes sure* **REV** *is out of earshot.*)

**BISCUIT.** Boy, you full of shit. Gimme another drink. I said-
ed what I wanted to say. *(beat)* Correctin' me an' shit.

(**ANDY** *pours him a drink.*)

**BISCUIT.** Yeah, there's your *difference.* All you education an'
shit, you still a nigger servin' a nigger.

**ANDY.** Things you believe –

**BISCUIT.** Tell me what to believe when you be walkin' in *my*
skin, lookin' in *my* mirror. Livin' *my* life.

**ANDY.** I hear ya.

**BISCUIT.** That's a good one.

**ANDY.** Don't wanna get into a whole thing, Biscuit.

**BISCUIT.** Know I'm right.

**ANDY.** Not about being right or wrong. Just life.

**BISCUIT.** Oh, you tellin' me about *life.* College boy tellin'
me 'bout *life* an' shit! You tryin' to tell this brother
what it be like out there?

**ANDY.** My life is just as real as yours.

**BISCUIT.** Shit, you ain't lived no real life till you a nigger in
this here world.

(**BISCUIT** *sits.* **CURTIS** *joins him.*)

CURTIS. Tell you I'm givin' notice?

BISCUIT. Yeah.

CURTIS. Think I should? I mean, I'm tired of baggin' them groceries alla time. Im 'a tell 'em. Friday's my last day. Friday's it. 'Cause I can get another job someplace else. Maybe Washington D.C?

*(CURTIS migrates upstage to talk to BILL.)*

BISCUIT. I hear they got good jobs over Washington, D.C. You think? 'Cause I'm tellin' 'em. I'm tired of baggin'…

*(ANDY cuts CURTIS off as he crosses downstage to BIS-CUIT.)*

ANDY. Think you're the only one that feels shit? You should have been a white guy on black Friday in my high school. Every Friday we had a riot. Once, I'm walkin' down the hall, this guy Danny Robertson grabs a fire extinguisher, slams it in my face. Blood everywhere. Thirty nine stitches later, they ask him why? " He's white." I look in the mirror, and see this scar, I think of him. I could look at every black guy and see Danny. I don't. That'd be stupid and ignorant. 'Cause he's a piece of shit punk, and although you're a bit of a blow hard racist fuck, you're good people.

BISCUIT. So we both lookin' at niggers in the mirror, huh?

ANDY. That how you see yourself?

BISCUIT. That's how it be.

*(Buzzer goes off. ANDY answers.)*

ANDY. Tenth Ward Club.

SPOOK. *(O.S.)* Spook.

*(He buzzes him in.)*

CURTIS. …'cause I got to make a move. Tired of baggin'. That's what I'm goin' do. Make a move.

*(SPOOK enters.)*

SPOOK. Guys. What's goin' on?

*(ANDY pours a beer sets it down.)*

**BISCUIT.** Conversatin' with this boy 'bout the real world out there.

**SPOOK.** It's a shithole.

**BISCUIT.** Thank you!

**ANDY.** You here?

**SPOOK.** No, I ain't.

*(SPOOK crosses to "his" chair. Sits.)*

**BISCUIT.** Do what you do to get by. Be pickin' up bodies for fourteen bucks an ass, I gonna say, "No sir, I ain't snatchin' up no dead folks." Nah, man. *(beat)* Shit. Tell you what you do. You be hopin' them motherfuckers dies on your shift since they just gonna die anyways.

**ANDY.** Morbid.

**BISCUIT.** Circle of life an' shit.

**ANDY.** You *wish* for people to die?

**BISCUIT.** How I pay the bills. Ain't wishin' death on none y'all, but it gonna happen. May as well be me baggin' yo' ass. For real. *(to SPOOK)* Sound like my nephew, Shawn. Opinions out the ass, ain't done shit yet.

**SPOOK.** How's Chloe?

**BISCUIT.** She good. Real good.

**SPOOK.** Still over Dollar General?

**BISCUIT.** Mm-hum. Tryin' to get Shawn in, too.

**SPOOK.** Over there?

**BISCUIT.** Keep him occupied. Nothin' permanent or nothin'. 'Times he be like his old man.

**SPOOK.** Who's his old man?

**BISCUIT.** Flattop. 'Member that crossed eyed junkie used to hang down at the Two Hundred club?

**SPOOK.** With the pan face?

**BISCUIT.** Why they call him Flattop an' shit. Fry an egg on that Motherfucker's head. *(beat)* He dead now.

**SPOOK.** Juice?

**BISCUIT.** That be the way. Bagged him myself. Back of Memphis Smoke. Heart attack. Bust his head open on the toilet. Like forty an' shit.

**SPOOK.** Young.

**BISCUIT.** True that.

*(Silence, then:)*

**CURTIS.** That's what I'm goin' do. I'm givin' notice. Tomorrow.

**SPOOK.** Grandfather went young, too. Woke up one morning, just felt tired. Cancer. Day he passed, father took me to Big Boy's. I was like ten. Sat me down inna booth. Looked at me, said, "My father is gone." All he said the whole meal.

**CURTIS.** Kind of shit's tough when you're little. In a way, I'm glad my old man left when I was a kid. Didn't get to know him, or see him get old and shit. Seen his picture, though. My mom keeps it buried in her bottom drawer. One time, I was baggin' this guy's groceries an' he looked like the picture. Just like it. Started to ask him if it was him, then I thought, if he wanted to know me, he'd of stayed. So, I just handed him his stuff and he walked away.

**SPOOK.** My dad was there, but not for long. Hit the death jackpot. No pain. Just went. 'Bout my age now. Drivin' on Euclid, hits a telephone pole. Bam! That's how I wanna go –

*(**BISCUIT**'s pager goes off.)*

**BISCUIT.** Sounds like fourteen dollars.

*(He starts to leave.)*

**SPOOK.** Comin' Sunday? Lions, Bills.

**BISCUIT.** Still preseason, man.

**SPOOK.** *Next to last* preseason game.

**BISCUIT.** Ain't goin' be playin' nobody good.

**SPOOK.** Starters playin' least first half.

**BISCUIT.** I feel ya. See, thing is, me an' Shawn be in the studio, recording.

**ANDY.** Wait, what are you guys doin'?

*(**BISCUIT** tries to ignore **ANDY**'s question, instead staying focused on **SPOOK**.)*

**BISCUIT.** Like I was sayin', Shawn –

**ANDY.** No, really?

**BISCUIT.** Shit you wouldn't know 'bout. Hip Hop.

(ANDY *busts out laughing.*)

**ANDY.** Ain't you a little old for that, Grand Pa?

**BISCUIT.** – Motherfucker! I got this right here *(points to his heart).* This all I need. Shit I seen? My words. Shawn's music. Tellin' ya. Our ticket out this here mess.

**ANDY.** Good luck.

**BISCUIT.** Fuck you.

**SPOOK.** Anyway…Sunday?

**BISCUIT.** Try, but got the studio for free. Lay that shit down, put it right on the internet.

**CURTIS.** "MySpace."

**BISCUIT.** There you go, that's right. Hookin' me up with this producer cat, Robert Bacon.

**SPOOK.** He good?

**BISCUIT.** Shit, yeah. An' he love what I be writin'. Young brother got an eye for talent. He be up an' comin'. Be like the Vince Young of hip – hop, my brother.

**SPOOK.** Huh…

**BISCUIT.** Shawn stay out of trouble, we gonna be doin' some real sweet shit. Talented. Talkin' 'bout goin' to L.A.

**SPOOK.** La-la land? What's he gonna find there, ain't here? This is Motown.

**BISCUIT.** My brother, Motown left here a long time ago.

*(He exits.)*

*(Lights fade out. In the blackout we hear baseball play by play which continues as the lights rise.)*

### The 10th Ward Club – Saturday Afternoon – Week Before Opener – August 31, 2007

*(SPOOK, GAIL, CURTIS and BILL are at the club.)*

*(Behind the bar is LENNIE, a no nonsense, burly man in his 40s. He hands LARRY a beer. LARRY moves downstage, keeping an eye on the TV.)*

SPOOK. Gail, Farve sucks!

GAIL. Yeah, I wish the Pack had a future hall of fame quarterback like Jon Kitna leading them.

SPOOK. Farve's done. Threw more picks last year than anyone in the league.

LARRY. Including Culpepper. What happened to that guy?

SPOOK. Lost Moss. Moss left, he was done.

CURTIS. Hear what Kitna predicted yesterday?

GAIL. What a dumbass. Ten wins.

LARRY. Watch.

GAIL. Maybe this decade, not this year.

SPOOK. Jackasses were eight an' eight and you're cackling? Tellin' you...and shut up, Gail. Tellin' you, this is our year –

GAIL. Please, every year, Spook.

SPOOK. Listen to me for once. Different this time. Tellin' you. Team's focused. Running game is developing. Coach Marinelli is restoring discipline. Everybody's in camp. Now they signed Calvin Johnson! So shut the fuck up! *(beat)* Wanna beer?

GAIL. No, thanks.

*(SPOOK goes to the bar. LENNIE pours him a beer.)*

LARRY. Ya know Calvin's agent is an old friend of ours.

GAIL. Really?                    CURTIS. Oh, yeah?

LARRY. Artie Piro.

GAIL. He's from around here?

LARRY. Went to school with us. Comin' to town next week.

GAIL. Gonna see him?

**LARRY.** Never too close with him. John was, though. You an' Artie, like two nuts in a sac, huh?

**SPOOK.** Pretty much. But I haven't seen him in over twenty years.

*(beat)*

**CURTIS.** *(to LARRY)* Think I'm goin' to North Carolina… D.C, Someplace like that. Not even givin' notice, Just goin' walk in there an' you know…that'll be it.

**LARRY.** We'll miss you.

*(LARRY walks over and sits next to GAIL. After a beat, CURTIS follows.)*

*(SPOOK crosses to the pool table and leans against the wall.)*

*(Flashback. The year is 1982.)*

*("Tush" by ZZ Top, or similar music\* plays as the lights rise on the pool table and dim on the club.)*

*(ARTIE PIRO, enters. In his early 20s, he is dressed in a business suit. He and SPOOK are in the middle of a pool game.)*

**ARTIE.** "…says, "Artie, I really appreciate this. Really." An' I say, "Appreciation don't put nothin' in my front pocket. Let's see some scratch."

**SPOOK.** No shit!

**ARTIE.** Fuck 'em. Everything got a price, Johnny.

**SPOOK.** Guess.

**ARTIE.** Yeah. Fuck, yeah. *(beat)* How you doin'?

**SPOOK.** Good. Real good.

**ARTIE.** Nice. Know, I haven't seen you in what? Four, five years?

**SPOOK.** Since 76', so six years.

**ARTIE.** Six years? Wow. But, it's like I talked to you yesterday. You don't change. *(off his reaction)* I mean that in a good way.

**SPOOK.** Thanks.

**ARTIE.** Know who did change? Lori Palm.

\* See MUSIC NOTE on page 3

**SPOOK.** Where'd you –

**ARTIE.** – What happened to her? She looks –

**SPOOK.** Drinks too much. All she does is drink an' collect welfare checks.

**ARTIE.** Ooohhh…

**SPOOK.** I look at her, I think, "Get a job, already." How tough can it be?

**ARTIE.** Nice. *(beat)* So what's this "Spook" shit?

**SPOOK.** Guys over Elias started callin' me Spook 'cause I'd always disappear on certain jobs…so, Spook…like Casper the ghost an' shit.

**ARTIE.** I'll stick with Johnny.

**SPOOK.** Call me asshole, just get your point across.

**ARTIE.** Asshole.

**SPOOK.** There ya go!

*(They share a laugh.)*

**SPOOK.** …two, side. *(misses)* Fuck me in the ass.

**ARTIE.** So how *are* things at the screw factory?

**SPOOK.** Elias is great! Just got promoted. Was workin' the press, but now I oversee them an' 'at.

**ARTIE.** Wearin' a tie?

**SPOOK.** No, fuck that. I ain't no suit. *(beat)* Nothin' personal.

**ARTIE.** I get it.

**SPOOK.** Seventy five cent an hour raise. Two weeks vacation. Five sick days a year. Weekends, most holidays off. Paid. Twelve bucks an hour. Back in school who'd a thought I'd be makin' that kind a cash?

**ARTIE.** Nice.

**SPOOK.** Best thing is…I always got a case of beers inna backseat, and a bag of pot inna glove.

**ARTIE.** Important.

**SPOOK.** Laugh, but it is.

**ARTIE.** I'm not laughing…it is. *(beat)* So, what else? Still followin' the Lions?

**SPOOK.** This is our year, man. Big tailgate party before the game Sunday. Wanna come by?

**ARTIE.** Thanks, but I'm gone tomorrow.

**SPOOK.** Fast.

**ARTIE.** Business. Time is money, and all that shit.

**SPOOK.** Fuckin' suit.

**ARTIE.** Blow me, mister twelve bucks an' hour an' paid holidays.

**SPOOK.** Right. So what exactly you doin' now? Sports management or somethin'?

**ARTIE.** A-S-M. American Sports Management. Did an internship. A lot of work for little or no pay, but the perks are great. Meet a lot of players. Agents. Like that.

**SPOOK.** Like?

**ARTIE.** Like Dor-sett?

**SPOOK.** Tony Dorsett?

**ARTIE.** Pronounces it Dor-sett, now.

**SPOOK.** Huh?

**ARTIE.** Incredible fuckin' asshole, too.

**SPOOK.** No!

**ARTIE.** Yeah.

**SPOOK.** Fuck me! You met Tony Dorsett?

**ARTIE.** Used to like the prick.

**SPOOK.** Sucks. Who else?

**ARTIE.** Bruce Smith.

**SPOOK.** No!

**ARTIE.** Matt Millen.

**SPOOK.** Matt fuckin' Millen? From the Raiders!?

**ARTIE.** Yeah.

**SPOOK.** Tell me he's a good guy –

**ARTIE.** Yeah, he's okay. Know who's really nice? Billy Sims.

**SPOOK.** Our Billy Sims!?

**ARTIE.** How many are there?

**SPOOK.** Yeah, just…wow. So fuckin' jealous. Kill to be in your shoes.

**ARTIE.** Yeah?

**SPOOK.** Fuck, yeah.

**ARTIE.** It's a lot of hard work, but yeah…the perks are sweet. Long hours, boss is kind of a dick…

**SPOOK.** Still. Billy Sims. Matt Millen.

**ARTIE.** Problem is, guys don't know shit about sports. Know business…but not sports.

**SPOOK.** Huh.

**ARTIE.** An' in order to make money. *Real* money. You gotta know sports. Know sports, the money comes rollin' in.

(**ARTIE** *pulls out a wad of money, and peels off a twenty. He notices* **SPOOK** *eyeing the cash.*)

**ARTIE.** Chump change, John. Grab us a couple. You fly, I'll buy.

(**SPOOK** *sets his beer on the pool table and reaches for the money.*)

**ANDY.** Hey!

(*Lights abruptly shift back to present time.*)

**ANDY.** You know better than that. Off the felt.

(*Suddenly,* **SPOOK** *looks up at* **ANDY.** **ARTIE** *is gone.* **ANDY** *exits.*)

**BILL.** Andy's a good bartender.

**SPOOK.** Fuck's so hard about bartendin' inna club, Bill? Pouring dollar drafts and shots.

**LARRY.** (Take it) easy.

**SPOOK.** What? I'm just sayin' what's so hard about it? And get outta my chair.

**LARRY.** *(mocking)* Sure, your majesty…!

(**SPOOK** *tosses* **LARRY** *out of his chair.*)

(**LENNIE** *crosses down looking for something. He spots* **CURTIS** *reading his magazine. He grabs it from him.*)

**LENNIE.** See ya, guys.

(*He leaves. Goodbyes.*)

**BILL.** Andy always keeps the pretzel bowls full. Lennie don't. Cheap. Think he owned the club, 'steada workin' here.

See? Nothin' but salt. Ha! Nothin' but salt.

(BILL *shakes the empty dish in front of* SPOOK*'s face.*)

SPOOK. Get that fuckin' thing out of my face!

BILL. Andy'll put somethin' out. You'll see. Goin' to school for business. Why he's a good bartender.

GAIL. Community college?

BILL. Yeah, Henry Ford. Got a program for guys been laid off around here.

SPOOK. Must be bustin' at the seams, then.

GAIL. 'Bout the only place. So slow over Shorty's, sendin' us home early most every day.

LARRY. I stopped openin' in the day, business is so slow. Wasn't for the specials I run...

SPOOK. Who's eatin' out? Know we ain't.

LARRY. Told Lefty he gets busy call me. Ain't called once.

(LARRY *crosses to bar phone. Makes a call.* ANDY *emerges from the back.*)

BILL. (*reading from the paper*) Hey...Lampert's got Starkist Tuna on sale 39 cents a can. Limit 4.

GAIL. That's good.

BILL. Oh, sale ends Wednesday. Limit 4. Curtis, when's the next sale start?

CURTIS. Huh?

BILL. Your sale. When's it start?

CURTIS. Circular comes out Tuesday, sale starts Wednesday. This'll be my last. Done with that place.

BILL. I'm tired.

CURTIS. My mother says I should stay put.

BILL. Didn't get any sleep last night.

CURTIS. You tired?

BILL. Um-hum.

CURTIS. You look tired, too.

BILL. Well, I am.

(ANDY *sets out a bowl of pretzels.*)

**BILL.** Aha! Pretzels!

(**LARRY** *hangs up.*)

**LARRY.** You know what? Bring him over.

**SPOOK.** Who?

**LARRY.** Artie.

**SPOOK.** We'll see. Probably busy, but, I'll see.

(**ANDY** *grabs the remote.*)

**ANDY.** Hey, the number!

(*From the TV, the "Daily Number" theme is heard. Every-one pulls out their ticket. With the exception of* **LARRY** *and* **SPOOK,** *they fall silent, staring at the screen.*)

**LARRY.** Bring him over the pizza shop. I'll make him some-thin' special.

**SPOOK.** We'll see!

**ANNOUNCER.** *(V.O.)* Let's play the Michigan Lottery. Live, this Saturday, August 31st, 2007. Thanks to today's witness Lili Spicer. And now today's Daily Number… the first digit is….three…the second digit…eight… and the third digit is…one. Today's winning big three number is 3-8-1.

**LARRY.** Shit. Had 3-8-2.

(*lights shift to –*)

### Waite Home – A Few Days Later

(**SPOOK** *crosses over during "The Number" and paces the floor. His wife* **BETH** *sits in a chair. An attractive woman in her 40s, she seems to carry the weight of the world on her shoulders. They're in mid conversation.*)

(*In the background, barely audible, a radio tuned to a classic rock station plays "Brave Strangers" by Bob Seger.\**)

**SPOOK.** Artie loves to gab. Yap, yap, yap, yap, yap. *(beat)* What am I goin' say, Beth?

**BETH.** Dunno.

**SPOOK.** Over twenty years.

**BETH.** Catch-up.

**SPOOK.** All a sudden when he's on top?

**BETH.** Maybe he'd like to hear from you.

**SPOOK.** That the kind of guy I am? Kind of *friend* I am?

**BETH.** John, he was your *best* friend!

**SPOOK.** No. I'm not callin' him now.

**BETH.** John –

**SPOOK.** Ship has sailed.

**BETH.** Then –

**SPOOK.** No.

**BETH.** No? You didn't even let me say what I wanted to say.

**SPOOK.** I know what you're gonna say.

**BETH.** Readin' minds, now?

**SPOOK.** Yeah, I am.

**BETH.** Instead of readin' minds, how about readin' the want ads?

**SPOOK.** Funny.

**BETH.** I'm not joking.

**SPOOK.** Well, I'm tryin', so…

**BETH.** Bank called again yesterday.

**SPOOK.** Told you, don't pick it up.

**BETH.** Called twice.

\* See MUSIC NOTE on page 3

**SPOOK.** I'll drop somethin' by this week.

**BETH.** With what?

**SPOOK.** Check day tomorrow.

**BETH.** That's the last one we got comin', and that'll take care of the car, but we got the house due, too.

**SPOOK.** How 'bout your check?

**BETH.** I'm gettin' the food an' regular bills with that.

**SPOOK.** Just don't pick up, they call. Stop down the bank, pay the car note in person.

**BETH.** Two months.

**SPOOK.** Whatever. Just don't pick up.

**BETH.** Two months late. Check ain't gonna cover two months.

**SPOOK.** Don't worry.

**BETH.** Jesus.

*(She moves away from him.)*

**SPOOK.** Rough patch is all. We been down this road before, right? The heater? Thing in the cellar? Katie's medical? We got through all of that. *(SPOOK goes over and takes her in his arms.)* We got married I couldn't give you nothin' but the promise to provide for you an' kids, if we was lucky enough to have 'em. I been doin' that. *(beat)* Okay. So. Got the wind knocked outta me a little lately, is all. Honest, I been tryin' –

**BETH.** Just keep fallin' further an' further behind.

*(He kisses her softly. She returns the kiss. It begins to get passionate. Just then, "Lights" by Journey\* comes on the radio. SPOOK pulls back and smiles.)*

**SPOOK.** Heard that on the stereo first time I saw you. To this day, I hear that song…*(beat)* Pourin' a beer at Nushwander's graduation party. I looked up an' saw you. Said to Nush, who the fuck is that!? Had them brown short pants on with that yellow tube top with those clogs of yours. Jeez. *(beat)* Moment I saw you, all I wanted to do was take care of you. Even back then. All I ever wanted. *(beat)* 'Member callin' you. So nervous.

\* See MUSIC NOTE on page 3

Heart poundin' so loud I swore you heard it through the phone. 'Member that first time we went out?

**BETH.** Nope.

**SPOOK.** Shit, you don't.

**BETH.** Don't.

**SPOOK.** Serious!?

*(She shrugs, pretending not to remember. He tickles her playfully.)*

**SPOOK.** Seriously don't remember first time we went out!

*(She squeals with laughter and surrenders.)*

**BETH.** "Heaven Can Wait." Eastland theatre. Me, you, Val DeFelice and Jennifer Grott. *(beat)* Remember my father that night?

**SPOOK.** Sam. Like to have seen his face 'fore I went up there. How'd I know I had to come up and knock on the door? Honkin' the horn.

**BETH.** Thank god for Val, huh?

**SPOOK.** Wasn't for him, I'd still be sittin' in the LeMans waitin'. *(beat)* Easier back then.

**BETH.** Guess.

**SPOOK.** No guessin' 'bout it, hon. Was.

**BETH.** John. Nothin' wrong with reachin' out. People reached out to us. And I can't help but think if Artie knew we needed help –

**SPOOK.** Beth…

**BETH.** No, John. Listen! Remember how good you felt helpin' Will Franklin? Dutch Shample? Everybody gets a turn. Good and bad. Our turn now. Call Artie, John. *(beat)* Can't sit in that LeMans forever.

*(**BETH** takes him in her arms and gently kisses him.)*

Come to the door now, sweetie. Ring the bell.

*(FADE OUT)*

## 10th Ward Club – Season Opener – Early September

*(LIONS (1-0)*

**TV ANNOUNCER.** *(O.S.)* It's the start of the N.F.L season and if Jon Kitna had a scratch off list for his number of guaranteed wins, it just went from 10 to 9! Lions! A 36-21 win. In Oakland! And for the first time in a looong while, I can say- the Lions are 1-0!

*(As the lights come up,* **SPOOK, LARRY, BILL, BISCUIT** *and* **CURTIS** *are celebrating the win.* **ANDY** *is behind the bar.)*

*(***REV** *enters, shot out of a cannon.)*

**REV.** My brothers! My brothers! My brothers! Did you see his work today? Of course you did. I knew it, I knew it, I knew it! I saw it in a vision! As I lay sleeping, I had a vision. I had a vision from the Lord. In this vision, the Lord said, "Reverend Russell Stuvants, my son…*he* is coming. He is coming to save you, and you, and you, and all long suffering Lions fans!!! I was paralyzed. My lips could not move. Finally, I gathered the strength to speak. And I whispered…who? And The Lord pulled back a silver and Honolulu blue curtain. And behind that curtain stood a powerful, bald, white man. A good, God fearing bald white man. A righteous bald white man. A bald white man with a cannon for an arm by the name of Jon Kitna! Jon Kitna! A true Christian and warrior. As soon as I saw him, I knew he would lead us. And he did lead us, did he not?

**SPOOK.** Sayin' you never seen Kitna before today?

**REV.** Not like this…no, no, no, no, no. Not like this.

**SPOOK.** Right.

**LARRY.** Rev realizes Kitna's part of a grand plan. Millen's plan.

**SPOOK.** Why even say his name? We're havin' a good time.

**LARRY.** Who? Millen?

**SPOOK.** Seriously. Larry, don't say it again.

**LARRY.** Gotta give him credit.

**SPOOK.** Got lucky with Kitna…Calvin Johnson was a no brainer. Hell, even Andy coulda drafted Johnson.

**LARRY.** But Millen brought them here.

**SPOOK.** And?

**LARRY.** He's responsible for that. Think they just showed up one day?

**SPOOK.** One day? How long it take for one day to come?

**LARRY.** Buildin' a team don't happen overnight.

**SPOOK.** Millen's been here what? Six, seven years?

**LARRY.** So?

**SPOOK.** What's a General Manager make?

**LARRY.** Not the point.

**SPOOK.** Oh, no? Makin' a lot for doin' shit. For what? What!? This plan!? You're a boob. He drafts Roy Williams first round...okay player, that's all, Not a franchise guy. Drafts Mike Williams. He's off smokin' a bowl in Oakland somewheres –

**LARRY.** How about Johnson?

**SPOOK.** Jury's out. Played one game.

**LARRY.** You love Calvin –

**SPOOK.** Sure, but how many times can you screw up? Had four top ten draft picks in five years. What would Dungy or Belichick, one of them guys'd do with that many number one's? And he's makin' millions. Millions! See him worryin' 'bout milk, gas prices, an' alla that shit!?

**REV.** Why?

**SPOOK.** Why what?

**REV.** Why are you angry? They *won* today.

**SPOOK.** Yeah, but –

**REV.** No, no, no. No "buts." The Detroit Lions won their season opener. On the road! Think about that. That's right...go ahead...*indulge.* The Detroit Lions won their season opener.

**SPOOK.** Right, Rev. We won.

**LARRY.** We won, pal.

**SPOOK.** Yeah. We won.

**REV.** Amen.

*(BLACKOUT)*

## 10th Ward Club – October 1

*(LIONS (3-1))*

*(SPOOK, REV, LARRY, CURTIS and BILL are in the club. ANDY is behind the bar.)*

**TV ANNOUNCER.** "…Coach Rod Marinelli after the team's thirty seven, twenty seven win over Chicago yesterday. This improves their record to three and one and keeps them right behind the Packers, knocking on the door to first place."

**REV.** Three and one! Yes, sir. Three and one!

**CURTIS.** *(beat)* only thing is I got that good health here. Think them places in D.C an' 'at, got good health, too?

**BILL.** I don't know. Guess it depends.

**CURTIS.** On what?

**BILL.** I dunno.

**LARRY.** Speakin' of health…Heard Moose stopped payin' his guys health over Perino's.

**REV.** No kiddin'.                    **SPOOK.** No shit?

**LARRY.** That's what Chinky Vaughn said, an' he's over there, so…

**SPOOK.** Never woulda happened if Feeg was still alive.

**CURTIS.** That's Moose's uncle, right?

**BILL.** Yeah.

**LARRY.** Can't handle the premiums. Said that, or close up.

**REV.** Lord have mercy!

**LARRY.** Less than five years, blew through all that cash his Uncle left him –

**BILL.** Feeg worked like a dog, for what?

**LARRY.** Generous fuck, but he never pissed around when there was work to be done.

**BILL.** Never missed mass. Every week he'd throw a hundred dollar bill in the basket. *(beat)* Always had a piece of fruit in his jacket. Handin' out apples, pears an' 'at.

**LARRY.** An' Moose don't even go to church no more, huh?

**BILL.** Not after his Uncle died.

**LARRY.** Too busy partyin'.

**BILL.** Guess.

**SPOOK.** Broad he's got on the side will leave him now, watch.

**LARRY.** Shit, yeah. Those guys over there are fucked. Chinky, Krohe an' them. Hell, Krohe's been workin' that dock forever. Now he needs it, he don't got health?

**ANDY.** Hear he's gotta get a colonoscopy.

**LARRY.** Who?

**ANDY.** Ed Krohe.

**LARRY.** He sick?

**ANDY.** Don't know. Gotta get one though.

**BILL.** I got a colonoscopy last year.

**LARRY.** *(sotto)* Colorado Bob.

**BILL.** Huh?

**ANDY.** Nothin'. He didn't say nothin'.

**LARRY.** Bet you liked that.

**SPOOK.** Probably went back for seconds.

**BILL.** Ha! Ha!

**LARRY.** Seriously, I give him three, four months, he closes.

**SPOOK.** Big shot, right?

**LARRY.** Produce ain't the same either. Still get my stuff there, but I ain't orderin' as much, way things are.

**REV.** What'd Feeg leave him?

**SPOOK.** Digger said the estate was worth a couple million –

**LARRY.** How's he know?

**SPOOK.** Wife works downtown.

**LARRY.** Speakin' of that. Been down there lately?

**SPOOK.** No.

**LARRY.** Like fuckin' Bagdad. Michigan Avenue. Wyoming.

**SPOOK.** Plant Re-opens? Things'll change. You'll see.

**LARRY.** *(beat)* Ain't comin' back, Spook.

**SPOOK.** Eventually they'll have to. Somethin' will move in there an' they'll need workers. *(awkward moment. REV starts to go.)* This is where stuff is made, remember?

*(BLACKOUT)*

## 10th Ward Club – October 28

*(LIONS (5-2))*

**ANNOUNCER.** *(V.O.)* Don't look now, but Jon Kitna's prediction is halfway right! He guaranteed 10 wins-The Lions are 5-2! Running back Kevin Jones had 105 yards rushing against the Bears, but with four interceptions, Detroit does it with defense.

*(SPOOK and BILL are celebrating the victory.)*

**SPOOK.** Sweet!

**BILL.** That Chicago is tough. I thought they would win for sure.

**SPOOK.** 'Cause you don't know football. It all started with that first pick by Griese.

**BILL.** I guess.

**SPOOK.** No guessin'. Their quarterback, Griese? I knew from his past, he was susceptible to the big pick. Throwing into double coverage was always his Achilles heel. Has the arm. Toughness. Pedigree. Just not smart.

*(SPOOK exits to restroom, as REV and CURTIS enter. Their dialouge should overlap.)*

**CURTIS.** Been talkin' to my mom about it and she wants me to stay put.

**REV.** Listen to your mother, Curtis.

**CURTIS.** You don't know what it's like. Every day, the same thing.

**REV.** *(beat)* I have an idea.

**CURTIS.** I see them places on the Travel Channel, right? Sometimes I just wanna get on a Greyhound bus and go.

**REV.** Maybe you should.

*(As REV and CURTIS move downstage.)*

**CURTIS.** Maybe, 'cause when I'm baggin them groceries? I see a pack of cookies or something, say? I look where

they're made and think of all the people workin',
makin' them. Who are these people? What are they
like? I'd like to meet them. Talk to them. But there I
am. Stuck baggin' at Lamperts.

*(SPOOK re-enters.)*

**SPOOK.** ...why he didn't stick in Denver, either! Remember
he was the heir to Elway?

**BILL.** I guess.

*(The buzzer goes off.)*

**ANDY.** Tenth Ward.

**LARRY.** Larry.

**SPOOK.** He was! He's bounced around. Denver, Tampa,
Chicago. A guy moves from team to team like that
somethin' wrong, see?

*(LARRY bursts in with a full head of steam, apron on
and a pizza in hand. He and Spook chest bump and
hug.)*

**LARRY.** Five and Two! Told you! Told you! I knew it! Five
and Two! Yeah! Hit my parlay.

**SPOOK.** Alright!

**LARRY.** Here's a housepie, guys!

*(They all thank him.)*

**SPOOK.** Hold on...!

**LARRY.** Can't.

**SPOOK.** Have a quick one.

**LARRY.** Busy as shit next door.

**SPOOK.** Well, thanks.

**LARRY.** Thank the Lions!

*(He leaves. They tear into the pizza, especially BILL.)*

**REV.** You believe we beat the Chicago Bears twice? Twice?

**SPOOK.** I do believe it. The way they're playin' Rev! And it's
to be expected with Marinelli 'cause he's a real disci-
plinarian.

**REV.** Yes, sir.

*(Spook crosses to the pizza, takes a slice and sits in his chair. REV moves downstage eating a slice. CURTIS tracks him down again.)*

**CURTIS.** Really. 'Cause I can't keep baggin' them groceries.

**REV.** Curtis, I don't mean to be rude but...

**CURTIS.** No, I know. But it's the same thing every day. *(REV moves away)* Listen to this, Rev. Listen. Okay? Listen. I asked if I could do somethin' else and Garlow said they needed me baggin'. Talkin' about, I was "the best bagger they had." Tired of it. You ever have to bag?

**REV.** Can't say as I have.

**CURTIS.** Lucky.

**REV.** I am lucky. I am blessed. I found my calling when I was a boy. My father passed away from heart disease as a very young man. I was so angry at the Lord that I demanded to know why he would steal from my mother and her five children, see, I have three brothers and a sister... why he would steal from us such a righteous, honest hard-working, God-fearing man like my father.

**CURTIS.** I always hear that "God fearing." Supposed to love God, not fear him, right?

**REV.** Love him, but also fear the almighty power he has. But I...at the age of eleven was ready to challenge that power.

**CURTIS.** Mad?

**REV.** Beside myself. Walked up to Reverend Brown, looked him in the eye and said,"I hate God. I hate you. And I want my father back."

**CURTIS.** Wow.

**REV.** He took me in his arms, held me tight and said, "Son, I feel your pain. World ain't always right, world ain't always fair, and I ain't got the answers for you. But I can tell you this. The good Lord needed a great man to lead his people in heaven, so he called on your father for assistance. He took him because he knew... he knew you had the strength to lead your family here on earth."

**CURTIS.** That fixed ya? What he said?

**REV.** No. It was how he said it. Looked me in the eye and talked to me. Talked to me. He made me feel whole. I came back the next day, and the next. His door was always open.

**CURTIS.** Hmm…

**REV.** He taught me there is no more noble purpose in life than to help your fellow man in times of great need and despair.

**CURTIS.** A lot of that 'round here.

**REV.** Son, you need to see the big picture. The Lord has surrounded us all with love and life. How can a man measure the beauty of life without a setback or two? Adversity is just a beast reminding us how wonderful things are when it is not present. These are all tests, Curtis. Tests.

*(beat)*

**CURTIS.** Baggin' at Lampert's is a test alright. I'm tired of it. How about Washington, D.C? Hear they got real good jobs there.

**SPOOK.** Curtis, will you shut up about that job?

**CURTIS.** Talkin' to Rev. So you shut up.

**SPOOK.** You ain't happy, quit. Just quit.

**CURTIS.** I am. Givin' notice on Friday.

**SPOOK.** Again? It's every week. Housepie?

**BILL.** *(beat)* I dunno. I just always figured somethin' came up.

*(CURTIS moves upstage, sits.)*

**SPOOK.** Jeez.

**BILL.** Just sayin' –

**SPOOK.** Drivin' me crazy…

*(SPOOK goes to the bar.)*

**REV.** John?

*(SPOOK reluctantly joins REV downstage. He motions for SPOOK to sit. He does.)*

**REV.** Talk to me, John.

**SPOOK.** What?

**REV.** I can see trouble written all over your face.

**SPOOK.** Guy drives me nuts.

**REV.** Boy don't mean no harm. Just unhappy in his job.

**SPOOK.** Least he's got a job. Lives at home. No mortgage. No responsibility, and he's bitchin'?

**REV.** Every cross has a different weight.

**SPOOK.** Huh.

**REV.** This life, while rewarding, can be trying. I know times are hard. Good you've such a strong sense of self. A lesser man would fall apart given your concerns.

**SPOOK.** Guess.

(**REV** *steps away, referencing the TV screen.*)

**REV.** Five and two!

**SPOOK.** Five an' two.

**REV.** Funny how life deals us all a different hand. Our boys being five and two. We feel so blessed with this fantastic start the good Lord has given us and yet, if we were in say, New England? We'd be wondering what in the world was wrong.

**SPOOK.** Weight of the cross, huh?

**REV.** Exactly.

**SPOOK.** An' New England's got that Spygate crap.

**REV.** Oh, most certainly! Caught cheating red handed. Wonder how that coach sleeps at night.

**SPOOK.** Seein' the broad he's sleepin' with, I'd say pretty good.

(**REV** *laughs and sits next to* **SPOOK.**)

**REV.** How are you sleeping, John?

**SPOOK.** Ah, you know...

**REV.** I understand your pressures. As I said before, you have a strong sense of self –

**SPOOK.** – cut to the chase, Rev. What's up?

(**REV** *hands him a business card.*)

**REV.** A friend. Mabel Johnson. Counselor at the Placement center.

**SPOOK.** Thanks, but I'm okay.

**REV.** She's expecting your call.

**SPOOK.** What you tell her?

**REV.** The truth. You're a proud man who could use a leg up. A man who could be of great assistance to the community's work force.

**SPOOK.** Huh.

*(**REV** gets up and crosses upstage to leave. He stops as he grabs and puts on his jacket.)*

**REV.** I have faith in you, John Waite.

*(**REV** leaves, **SPOOK** stares at the card.)*

*(Lights shift as **BETH** enters.)*

### Waite Home – The Next Morning – October 29

*(She sees* **SPOOK** *with card in hand.)*

**BETH.** Alright, I'm off to work now, sweetie.

**SPOOK.** Okay, bye baby..

**BETH.** Where are you goin'?

**SPOOK.** Got a nine o'clock appointment.

**BETH.** Where?

**SPOOK.** Don't wanna jinx it.

*(She extends her hand to see the card.* **SPOOK** *plays "keep away with it.")*

**BETH.** C'mon…

**SPOOK.** What?

**BETH.** Lemme see.

*(Finally, he hands it over.)*

**SPOOK.** Placement Center.

**BETH.** Really?

**SPOOK.** I don't know…

**BETH.** Can't hurt.

**SPOOK.** We'll see. I think it's bullshit, but…y'know. What the hell, right?

**BETH.** You're not goin' like that are you?

**SPOOK.** What?

**BETH.** Like that.

**SPOOK.** Why not?

**BETH.** It's an interview, not poker in the back of Larry's pizza shop.

**SPOOK.** I'm fine.

**BETH.** John.

**SPOOK.** Why I gotta dress up?

**BETH.** Respectful.

**SPOOK.** Kissin' ass.

**BETH.** You're right. Just wear your goddamn dirty Lions shirt and your jeans.

**SPOOK.** That's who I am.

**BETH.** Exactly. And that's the problem.

**SPOOK.** Findin' a lot of problems with me lately.

**BETH.** You don't know the half of it.

*(She starts off. He grabs at her.)*

**SPOOK.** Hey! The hell you goin'? I'm talkin' to you!

**BETH.** Hold on!

*(She brushes him off and exits, returns with a dress shirt and tie.)*

**BETH.** At least make an effort.

*(Hands him the items and exits. He looks them over, then tosses them aside. Lights shift to:)*

### Career Placement Center – Downtown Detroit – Later That Day

*(We are inside the workers placement center.* **MABEL JOHNSON,** *African-American, 50s, professional, sits in a chair.* **SPOOK,** *in his jeans and Lions shirt sits across from her.)*

*(Underneath, generic office noise is heard throughout the scene.)*

**MABEL.** College?

**SPOOK.** Nope.

**MABEL.** High school?

**SPOOK.** Finished.

**MABEL.** Wonderful.

**SPOOK.** Guess. I graduated, but from the voc-tech…

**MABEL.** I see.

**SPOOK.** But I still learned a lot in shop. So –

**MABEL.** Mr. Waite, I'm not judging you. I just need to know where you are, what you're qualified for.

**SPOOK.** 'Cause of shop? Always been good with my hands an' 'at.

**MABEL.** Repairs and such?

**SPOOK.** 'Sides working over Elias all them years, I done…I done all kinds a stuff. Humpin' beer, cleanin' an' layin' brick an' 'at. You know…regular work.

**MABEL.** No, that's excellent.

**SPOOK.** Got anything like that there?

*(She scans her paperwork.)*

**MABEL.** Humm…

**SPOOK.** …'Cause that's my strength…handy stuff.

**MABEL.** I understand. I do. Unfortunately this whole area has seen a shift away from the traditional style of labor needed to a more service oriented –

**SPOOK.** Service is good. I always been on time for work. Always ready to work. I'm great at service. Check my record...when it comes to service my record is good. Real good.

**MABEL.** Excellent. You've done a lot of odd jobs, I take it?

**SPOOK.** Yeah.

**MABEL.** Can you work a cash register?

**SPOOK.** Why I need to work a register?

**MABEL.** Most of these establishments are looking for cashiers.

**SPOOK.** That be inside?

**MABEL.** Inside where?

**SPOOK.** Inside the building an' 'at.

**MABEL.** Yes.

**SPOOK.** Huh.

**MABEL.** Mr. Waite? You *are* familiar with the service industry?

(*A pool of light appears behind* **MABEL,** *as* **ARTIE** *enters. He stands behind* **MABEL** *and addresses* **SPOOK.**)

**ARTIE.** It's a lot of hard work, but...yeah, the perks are sweet. Long hours, boss is kind of a dick–

**SPOOK.** Still. Billy Sims. Matt Millen.

**ARTIE.** Problem is, guys don't know shit about sports. Know business...but not sports.

**SPOOK.** Huh.

**ARTIE.** An' in order to make money. Real money. You gotta know sports. Know sports, the money comes rollin' in.

**SPOOK.** Sure.

**ARTIE.** Those business guys? Cocks. So, I'm opening my *own* management firm.

**SPOOK.** Wow.

**ARTIE.** I've seen the future of this business, and it is me.

**SPOOK.** Huh.

**ARTIE.** All you need is one good client to rep. You get the first, the rest just start comin'. Like pussy. Know how when you're fuckin' a broad steady, seems like pussy just lines up? Well, same in business. (*beat*) Met a guy A.S.M was interested in. Defensive end, big as a house, fast as shit. From this tiny, tiny school in the south. Plow boy type. Willie Anderson –

SPOOK. – Middle Tennessee State. Fuckin' stud. Ran a four-seven his junior year.

ARTIE. Damn…

SPOOK. Fell off the radar after he racked his knee. Baby Deacon, they called him baby Deacon 'cause he reminds people of Deacon Jones. Wasn't for that knee –

ARTIE. – only reason I got him. They lost interest. Not me. Been talkin' to him. Focused. Healthy. Gonna be a star. I can't believe you know him!

*(Lights shift back as Mabel resumes speaking.* ARTIE *exits. We are in the interview again. Present time.)*

MABEL. What I'm asking is, do you realize when I said "service" I was referring to *customer* service? Businesses that serve the needs of the public? Retail shops, Restaurants…that sort thing?

SPOOK. Oh, yeah. I knew…I knew that. Everybody does. I just thought…*(beat)* Honest. I didn't know what "service" meant. But I'm a real quick learner. I pick stuff up real fast. Anybody tell ya that.

MABEL. Mr. Waite…would you feel comfortable working in a convenience store or a restaurant?

SPOOK. That's service jobs, huh?

MABEL. Most are part time, with the added benefit of a flex schedule.

SPOOK. Part time? No. I need a real, full time job.

MABEL. I understand, but –

SPOOK. – you get health an 'at, part time?

MABEL. Some do. Most do not. Mr. Waite, in this new economy –

SPOOK. Got a family. Kid's grown, but I gotta wife.

MABEL. I understand. Maybe her job – ?

SPOOK. No, they don't. *(beat)* How can they have jobs with no benefits? Pricks. New economy? They can kiss my ass! *(beat)* Jeez. I'm sorry, excuse my language. Didn't mean that.

MABEL. It's okay.

**SPOOK.** Really, I'm sorry.

**MABEL.** I understand. You're frustrated. It's a bad system, but it's the only one we've got.

**SPOOK.** Well, thanks. Mind I think about it?

**MABEL.** Certainly. This program is here for you. We can help you with this transition.

**SPOOK.** Thanks.

(**MABEL** *exits.* **SPOOK** *is left alone on stage. He wears a look of concern. Suddenly –*)

**ANNOUNCER.** *(V.O.)* "Ramsey back to pass. Throws- Picked off! Shaun Rogers down the side line! At the thirty... twenty... fifteen... ten! Stiff arms a man and he's... into the end zone! Touchdown Detroit Lions!!!

(*As* **SPOOK** *stands there, mesmerized by the announcers call, the lights shift back to the club.*)

## 10th Ward Club – November 4

*(LIONS (6-2))*

*(Lions 44, Denver 7)*

*(ANDY, REV, BISCUIT, CURTIS and BILL enter with a burst of energy during the announcer's call.)*

**BISCUIT.** Shit, yeah. Baby! We on our way now!

**SPOOK.** Detroit Lions, yeah!

**REV.** This is a day to rejoice and thank the Lord. Thank the good Lord for watching over our boys in silver and Honolulu blue.

**BISCUIT.** Couple more wins-playoffs!

**CURTIS.** Can't believe we scored all them points!

**REV.** Lord have mercy!

*(The buzzer goes off. Through the following section, ANDY will try unsuccessfully to get SPOOK's attention. Everyone's dialogue should overlap and completely ignore him.)*

**REV.** Forty four to seven!

**BISCUIT.** Whoa! That sounds like a good number. I'm a play that tomorrow. Four-four-seven.

**REV.** Four-four-seven. Does have a certain ring. Play it for me, too.

*(REV hands him a some money.)*

**SPOOK.** We're goin' to the playoffs!

*(The room erupts.)*

**SPOOK.** The playoffs! Think of that! The playoffs! Us in the playoffs!

**ANDY.** Hey, Spook!

**REV.** Can you even imagine what this city will be like if do get there...?

*(The buzzer sounds again. ANDY answers, tries to get SPOOK's attention again.)*

**SPOOK.** No, Rev. No, no, no, no, no. No more "if's." It's –

**ALL.** When!

**SPOOK.** It's all positive. Hell, even Phil Simms is sayin' we're goin' to the playoffs. All jumpin' on the bandwagon. Everybody loves us now!

**ANDY.** Spook!

**REV.** Yes, indeed.

**SPOOK.** An' it wasn't just Kitna or Williams. Complete an' total team effort. Special teams, running game. Oh, man!

*(The buzzer goes off again. This time,* **ANDY** *crosses from behind the bar, looks to the outside doorway, then crosses downstage to* **SPOOK**.*)*

**CURTIS.** Kitna called it. Kitna called ten wins.

**REV.** And America laughed!

**SPOOK.** All thought he was crazy. I'll admit it now, but, honest, even I thought it was a reach.

*(***ANDY** *taps* **SPOOK** *on his shoulder.* **SPOOK** *ignores him.)*

**ANDY.** Spook! C'mere. Spook!

**SPOOK.** Shut up, Andy. We're celebratin' here!

**ANDY.** Spook!

*(***ANDY** *grabs* **SPOOK***'s arm with much greater urgency.* **SPOOK** *pushes him away.)*

**SPOOK.** Will you shut the fuck up!

*(***ANDY** *throws his hands in the air, crosses behind the bar, hits the buzzer.)*

**BISCUIT.** Lions goin' all the way, baby. I can feel it!

**CURTIS.** Know why they're winnin'? Everytime I fill a bag I say "Go, Lions"!

**REV.** Oh, no, no! I had that vision! Remember, I said I had that vision –

**SPOOK.** No, It's because Marinelli runnin' a disiplined –

**BISCUIT.** Shit. Everybody taking credit but the one's done it. The Lions done it y'all. They the reason –

*(***BETH** *storms in.)*

**BETH.** Hey!

*(The conversation comes to screeching halt as all eyes turn to her.)*

**BETH.** Ever gonna answer my calls?

**SPOOK.** What?

**BETH.** Called here three times.

**SPOOK.** Let's go outside.

**BETH.** No.

**SPOOK.** C'mon. Take a walk…

**BETH.** This is fine. Why? Embarrassed?

**SPOOK.** No. It's just. I can see you're mad about somethin' –

**BETH.** Goddamn right I'm mad.

**SPOOK.** Let's go outside.

**BETH.** No! I'm not going to be pushed aside like everything else in your life.

**SPOOK.** Keep your voice down?

**BETH.** And if I don't? Huh? What if I don't?

*(She bursts over to where the men are sitting and with one sweep of her foot, clears off the small coffee table. Pizza, newspapers, playing cards all go flying. She jumps on top of the table. The men make a beeline out of the club.)*

**SPOOK.** Stop it.

**BETH.** This is great. Finally got your attention. Huh? Should have thought of doin' this a long time ago.

*(Just then, **LARRY** runs in.)*

**LARRY.** I told you –

*(The sight of their confrontation stops him in his tracks.)*

**LARRY.** – Sorry.

*(He swiftly leaves.)*

**SPOOK.** C'mon, Beth. What do you want? You're embarrassing me here.

**BETH.** You want embarrassed, lemme fill ya in on my day. Our daughter stops by with this new guy. He seems real nice. Clean. Polite. Decent. Got a job. A man with a job? Wow! How could ya not love a man with a job? Right? Sittin' there havin' lunch an' we're havin' a great time. A great time. But then they get real quiet. I look out the front window and I see American Recovery towin' our car.

**SPOOK.** You're kiddin' –

**BETH.** Yeah, John. I'm *joshing* with you. Love coming down here to *josh* about shit like this.

**SPOOK.** During the game!

**BETH.** Right. Instead of watching the Goddamn Lions, they're working.

*(She pushes him.)*

**BETH.** Working! Making a living! What a concept, huh?

**SPOOK.** Alright.

**BETH.** They repossessed our car while you were sittin' here watchin' the game!

**SPOOK.** Talk to them tomorrow. Take care of it.

**BETH.** Too late! It's gone! They took it right in front of company.

**SPOOK.** Stop bein' so goddamn dramatic, it was just Katie.

**BETH.** This guy, too! The look on his face! On her face!

**SPOOK.** She'll understand. I'll talk to her. Now go home.

**BETH.** Home. What is *that*!? Think about the word, John. "Home." Think about it. Think about what we got over there and tell me if that's a "home."

**SPOOK.** You need to stop watching Oprah.

**BETH.** Yeah, and you need to do a lotta stuff. But you don't.

**SPOOK.** Stop this shit right now!

**BETH.** *(beat)* We need to talk when you come back tonight. Notice I didn't say "home." We gotta talk. Seriously sit down and talk.

*(She turns to go.)*

**SPOOK.** Go ahead. Say what you gotta say.

**BETH.** *(as she's leaving)* I can say a lot.

**SPOOK.** Say whatever you want. Sick of your shit…every goddamn day, naggin' me. *(BETH turns back)* Say whatever it is you're gonna say an' be done with it.

**BETH.** Alright. I want you to leave! When you get back tonight, I'll have your stuff packed. I want you to leave.

*(long pause)*

**SPOOK.** Ain't leavin' my own house.

**BETH.** So it's your house, now? Not ours? It's yours?

**SPOOK.** Yeah.

**BETH.** Hey! It's not like I woke up this morning and thought, "Today's the day, I'll leave John." I can't take it anymore. I see people like my sister and her husband, and I know they ain't perfect, but at least they're trying –

**SPOOK.** Beth.

**BETH.** – you stopped tryin'. Long time ago.

**SPOOK.** Hey –

*(He reaches out to touch her. She crosses away from him.)*

**BETH.** Don't you touch me. Don't you fucking touch me.

**SPOOK.** C'mon.

**BETH.** I'm never happy when I'm with you. *(beat)* Know my favorite time of the day? Workin' at the Dollar Store, 'cause at least I don't have to deal with this.

**SPOOK.** Don't love me no more?

**BETH.** I, I can't – *(beat)* Know what? Just…I'll go to my sister's for couple days till you find a place, but then –

**SPOOK.** C'mon…

**BETH.** Bye.

**SPOOK.** You're just gonna go?

**BETH.** Be at Sandy's.

*(She begins to leave.)*

**SPOOK.** Fuckin' bitch.

*(She stops dead in her tracks. Turns.)*

**BETH.** What did you say? *(SPOOK says nothing.)* You gotta get yourself together.

*(She exits. SPOOK is left alone. Picks up the remote, points it at the TV.)*

**TV ANNOUNCER.** …as the Lions trounce the Broncos forty four to seven and run their record to six and two! Six and two! And right there in the playoff hunt. Man! If you're a Lions fan you're on top of the world! From Ford Field this is Bob Thompson, channel 7 Action News. Nancy?

*(Lights fade.)*

**End of Act One**

# ACT TWO

### 10th Ward Club – Sunday Nov. 11

*(LIONS (6-3))*

*(***SPOOK*** *sits watching highlights of the game.* ***BISCUIT*** *has one eye on the TV, the other focused on his notepad, working on his lyrics. It is late.* ***ANDY*** *is taking out the trash, getting ready to close.)*

**TV ANNOUNCER.** The six and three Lions were held to an embarrassing minus eighteen yards and turned the ball over five times in falling to the Arizona Cardinals. Even so, at six and three they're still right there, as they prepare to face the Giants next week. Meanwhile –

*(***SPOOK*** *grabs the remote, mutes the sound.)*

**SPOOK.** Home.

**BISCUIT.** Come again?

**SPOOK.** Somethin' Beth was sayin'. Home. When you think of it, what you think of?

**BISCUIT.** Place. You know, where we live.

**SPOOK.** What do you do there, though?

**BISCUIT.** Huh?

**SPOOK.** Serious. Ain't fuckin' 'round.

**BISCUIT.** I feel you. *(beat)* Place we live.

**SPOOK.** Where you "live." Right.

**BISCUIT.** You gettin' all crazy an' shit on me, bro?

**SPOOK.** Know, Biscuit. Been thinkin' 'bout ninth grade. Decided to go academic. No more shop. This is big, 'cause 'member, only them Liberace motherfuckers went academic. Guys like us, take shop. *(beat)* I decided to switch to academic startin' in tenth grade. Political science an' math an' all that shit. Academic.

**BISCUIT.** Classes an' shit.

**SPOOK.** Goin' to hand in my schedule, an' I gotta take a piss. Bobby Harder's in the bathroom smokin' a joint. Gold. Paints the rolling paper with black hash oil, too. Fuckin' great buzz. Tremendous. Talkin' about a new

voc-tech shop. Building Maintenance. Supposed be
the best shop ever. Sounds like a big deal. Don't know,
somewhere between the Gold and Harder's bullshit,
I end up in Building Maintenance the tenth grade…
and the year after that. Graduated a janitor.

**BISCUIT.** Feel ya.

**SPOOK.** Could've been…I don't know. Not where I am
today.

**BISCUIT.** Way I sees it, we is who we is. We can think on how
it should be, what it should be, but end of the day?
This right here, is what it be.

**SPOOK.** What the fuck you talkin' about?

**BISCUIT.** Alright. Think you fucked yourself by not takin'
them classes an' shit. But who's to say you even cut out
for that there mold? Maybe you take that class, hate
the motherfuckin' shit an' drop out of school.

**SPOOK.** Guess.

**BISCUIT.** But this here? The moment right now? This here
livin'. Things tough. No doubt. But you amongst
friends, with much love for you, my brother.

**SPOOK.** All I ever wanted was to be a good husband and
father.

**BISCUIT.** And you is. Shit. Maybe it be her shit that's fucked
up right now.

**SPOOK.** Think?

**BISCUIT.** Like you been givin' only four cards in a game of
five card stud and you still tryin' to make the best of it.
You alright.

**SPOOK.** Almost hit her the other day.

**BISCUIT.** Did you?

**SPOOK.** Came close.

**BISCUIT.** If I had a dime every time I feel like smackin'
Andy upside his motherfuckin' head – ?

**SPOOK.** – he's an asshole. She's my wife.

**BISCUIT.** My brother, you need to stop bein' so hard on
yourself. Enough people out there gonna do it for

you. Don't need to lend them a hand.

SPOOK. Thanks.

(BISCUIT *watches* SPOOK *as he takes a long drink of his beer.*)

BISCUIT. Check it out, come over the crib tonight watch some TV with the kids. Get you out that basement for a night.

SPOOK. It's not that bad. *(beat)* Another time, not tonight. Take a rain check? (BISCUIT *nods.*) God bless ya, now get outta here.

(BISCUIT *leaves.*)

(lights shift as SPOOK crosses to-)

### Basement of Larry's Pizza Shop – Mid November

*(LIONS (6-4))*

**(SPOOK** *stumbles in, drunk. He sits on a small cot. Underneath, we hear the following audio:)*

**RADIO ANNOUNCER.** *(V.O.)* Well, they took it on the chin again today, falling to the New York football Giants sixteen to ten. The Lions are now six and four, and get ready to host the Green Bay Packers on Thanksgiving. And that's it for sports…

*(He pulls from his pocket a cell phone and dials.)*

**SPOOK.** Hello? Hello? Katie? Hey, honey. What are you doin' there?…That's good. Your mother there?…Let me ask you. Would you cry if I died? Would ya?…Don't. Don't cry if I die. *(beat)* My dad didn't cry when – Your mother won't cry 'cause she don't love me anymore. But I love her. Your mother. *(beat)* I do. You know your mother? Your mother. Your mother…your mother is a good woman…a good woman and a good wife and I love her. *(beat)* Can I talk to her, please?…When? Okay. *(beat)* Is she really not there, 'cause I need to talk to her…No, I know you wouldn't lie. But can I ask you to ask you to ask her to call me? *(beat)* 'Cause…I…

*(The phone drops from his hand as he begins to pass out. Falling asleep, he mutters:)*

**SPOOK.** Katie? Katie?

*(FADE OUT)*

## 10th Ward Club – Later That Day

*(In the dark, a news magazine program is heard. When the lights come up,* **ANDY** *is behind the bar intently watching.* **BILL** *is standing in front of his stool, shaking his leg.)*

**TV PANELIST #1.** *(V.O.)* "Ultimately, Americans will just have to work longer and put off their retirement."

*(Buzzer is heard.)*

**ANDY.** 10th Ward.

**SPOOK.** Spook. Open the fuckin' door.

**TV PANELIST #2.** *(V.O.)* "Is that fair?

**TV PANELIST #1.** What's fair? Hey, the days of the free rides are gone and if people can't deal with that, too bad."

**(SPOOK** *enters, still drunk and carrying the day on his back.)*

*(ANDY pours a beer for* **SPOOK.** *)*

**BILL.** Spook.

**TV PANELIST #1.** *(V.O.)* "...but is that fair? The American people have paid into this system for years –."

**TV PANELIST #2.** *(V.O.)* "Hold on. No one comes into this world with a guarantee that things will be easy."

**(SPOOK** *grabs the remote. Starts to channel surf.)*

**ANDY.** Hey! I'm watchin' that!

**SPOOK.** Fuck this shit.

**BILL.** My legs ain't worth a nickle today. *(He sits on his stool.)* Maybe new shoes. Think new shoes's will help?

**ANDY.** Maybe.

**BILL.** Before I forget. Half price candy tomorrow over Big Lots.

**ANDY.** Yeah?

*(Spook eventually comes across a Lions highlight show from 1997. The buzzer goes off.)*

**ANDY.** 10th Ward.

BISCUIT. *(V.O.)* Biscuit.

BILL. Yeah. Half Price. Gotta get there early for the good stuff. Snickers an' that.

ANDY. Good to know.

BILL. M&M's? I keep 'em in the freezer, last forever. Fifty percent off, can't beat that with a stick.

(**BISCUIT** *enters.*)

BISCUIT. Fellas!

BILL. Hey.

BISCUIT. 'Sup, my brother?

SPOOK. '97 highlights.

BISCUIT. You mean low-lights.

SPOOK. Kiddin'? Fuckin' great year. Barry two thousand yards. M.V.P an' 'at. 'Member how excited we all were?

BISCUIT. …'member losin' the wild card to ummm… ummm?

SPOOK. Tampa! Could've been worse. Think. In '42…went 0-11. Besides, how many other teams got to the play-offs? An' watchin' Barry do that?

BISCUIT. Um hum.

SPOOK. How dominant was this guy? Rushing record in '94…'97… Rookie of the year in '89. Why'd he quit?

BISCUIT. Got me.

(**BILL** *references the circular to* **ANDY**.)

BILL. Yep. Half price! Can't beat it!

BISCUIT. Huh?

SPOOK. …half price candy shit.

BISCUIT. Who got half price candies?

BILL. Big Lots. Tomorrow. Half price off all candy.

(**BISCUIT** *crosses to* **BILL**, *looking at his circular.*)

BISCUIT. They got Three Musketeers, Bill?

BILL. Got all kinds of stuff. Never know 'til ya get there.

BISCUIT. Bet they got Butterfingers an' shit, too.

SPOOK. Thing about Barry…how he could walk away from the all time rushing record, never mind all that cash.

**BISCUIT.** Housepie, you gonna to get some of that candy tomorrow?

**BILL.** Yeah.

**SPOOK.** Walkin' away from that kinda money. Wonder if he'd do it again?

**BISCUIT.** Guess we never know that shit. *(to* **BILL***)* They got them Three Musketeers, grab me some!

(**BISCUIT** *sits at the bar.*)

**BILL.** Oh, sure. If they got 'em. I'll look. Three Musketeers.

**BISCUIT.** Yeah.

**BILL.** Like that nougat, huh?

**BISCUIT.** New what?

**BILL.** Nougat. The secret of Three Musketeers. What makes 'em fluffy.

**BISCUIT.** Yeah, then I dig me some nougat.

**ANDY.** It's not nougat.

**BISCUIT.** Say what?

**ANDY.** "Nougat" is found in say, Snickers or Mars bars…but Three Musketeers has a marshmallow whip.

**BISCUIT.** Call it whatever you want, long as it's half off.

**BILL.** Yeah. They got them TV commercials with those pretty girls jumping up to catch the candy bars, but they're so light, because of the nougat –

**ANDY.** – it's not nougat!

**BILL.** Or whatever. They just fly away.

**SPOOK.** Think he regrets it?

**BISCUIT.** What?

**SPOOK.** Barry. Walkin' away from all that cash?

(*Lighting shifts to reveal* **ARTIE** *entering the center stage area, he sits next to* **SPOOK**.)

**ARTIE.** I can't believe you know him! Using my contacts from A-S-M, got him try-outs with Miami, Chicago and Pittsburgh.

**SPOOK.** Love to see him in the Pros.

**ARTIE.** Will be. Things happen the way I know they will? I'll be wipin' my ass with "fuck you money."

**SPOOK.** Right.

**ARTIE.** Johnny, you know football like nobody else I know.

**SPOOK.** I don't know.

**ARTIE.** I do. I got an offer for you. Grow this thing with me.

**SPOOK.** I'm not a business guy.

**ARTIE.** Don't matter. I can trust you. You know how invaluable trust is? Anyone can learn how to read a contract, add up numbers…but to have your eye *plus* be a man of his word? That's rare.

**SPOOK.** I don't know.

**ARTIE.** Opportunity, Johnny. Old fuck in New York wants to bankroll me. Found an office. Started the paperwork, all of that.

**SPOOK.** Yeah?

**ARTIE.** Puts up all the cash, I make it grow. Brassy fuck, but I run the show an' he knows it.

**SPOOK.** What I do?

**ARTIE.** Watch film. Go to games. Have an office cubicle. Everything.

**SPOOK.** Where?

**ARTIE.** New York.

**SPOOK.** New York!?

**ARTIE.** Where the gold is, buddy. Whaddya say?

**SPOOK.** I don't know. Kinda confused. Like…what about pay?

**ARTIE.** Now, that's the tough part. I'm not taking pay until we start showin' a profit, but since you'd technically be an employee, you'll get a starting salary, but that'll go up as we grow. And we *will* grow.

**SPOOK.** I don't know.

**ARTIE.** What's not to know? We'll be rich! So rich that assholes like that lawn guy that time, will never look down on us again.

**SPOOK.** Never forget that fat prick.

**ARTIE.** Fuckin' right. Me, too.

**SPOOK.** I felt that big.

**ARTIE.** How they want you to feel.

**SPOOK.** *(pause)* Gotta talk to my wife.

**ARTIE.** Nice! Talk to Beth. Fact, my mom wants yc
come over for dinner tomorrow night before l

**SPOOK.** I'll talk to her.

**ARTIE.** Because a guy like you! I mean, you knew a
Willie Anderson! That's fuckin'…fuck!

**SPOOK.** Baby Deacon? How could you not?

**ARTIE.** …be surprised, John.

**SPOOK.** Billy Sims, huh?

**ARTIE.** Billy fuckin' Sims. Tell you more over dinner.

*(ARTIE gets up to leave.)*

**ARTIE.** Want you on the team, Waite.

**SPOOK.** Thanks!

*(Standing in the doorway, ARTIE calls out.)*

**ARTIE.** Building a big moat in front of my castle, buddy.
Which side you goin' be on?

*(ARTIE exits the club, but remains in the back watching
SPOOK.)*

**SPOOK.** Yeah, well. I gotta talk to Beth.

**BISCUIT.** What?

*(Lights up abruptly on the club. Back to the present.)*

**SPOOK.** Huh?

*(BISCUIT takes him in.)*

**BISCUIT.** You cool, man?

**SPOOK.** Yeah. Just, ah…thinkin' about findin' a job, you
know?

**BISCUIT.** I feel you.

*(beat)*

**SPOOK.** How 'bout you guys?

**BISCUIT.** Come again?

**SPOOK.** Just thinkin'…if you guys needed help down
there –

**BISCUIT.** At the morgue?

**SPOOK.** Yeah.

**BISCUIT.** You don't wanna be workin' with no dead bodies.

**SPOOK.** Just thinkin' –

**BISCUIT.** Trust me. Ain't your thing.

**SPOOK.** They hirin'?

**BISCUIT.** No, man.

**SPOOK.** Gotta find somethin'.

**BISCUIT.** It'll come. Need to chill, bro.

**SPOOK.** Thing is, is…I was thinkin', if you, you know, could put in a word or two…

**BISCUIT.** Doin' what?

**SPOOK.** Anything. Baggin' –

**BISCUIT.** – don't *need* no more baggers, man.

**SPOOK.** C'mon –

**BISCUIT.** Past weekend I ain't had but two bodies. Two. That's twenty eight bucks the weekend. Whole weekend. 'Sides. You baggin' be cuttin' into my earnin' power…see what I'm sayin'?

**SPOOK.** You can't tell me there's nothin'. *Nothin'!*

**BISCUIT.** There's somethin', but that somethin', be taking food off my table. Nobody takin' food off my table. Friend, family, nobody. Shit, my cousin Tyrone asked me the same mess the other day, I told him no. *(beat)* What happened downtown?

**SPOOK.** Got these great *service* jobs. Know what *service* jobs are? Fuckin' Arby's an' shit for eight bucks an hour. "Hi. Can I take your order?" Alla that shit. I need some income.

**BISCUIT.** What you think morgue be payin'?

**SPOOK.** I need somethin'. Anything.

**BISCUIT.** Hear you –

**SPOOK.** No you don't. You don't! Or you'd talk to them for me. You'd –

**BISCUIT.** What? What? Give you half of my twenty eight dollars so both our families can starve? Shit, man. We boys, an' all that an' I know you goin' through some shit, but I ain't your daddy. Act like a man, boy! Get your shit together. We all got problems…

*(**ARTIE** in the doorway, calls out to **SPOOK**.)*

**ARTIE.** How they want you to feel. That big.

**SPOOK.** Yeah.

**BISCUIT.** ...can't be snifflin' like no bitch.

(SPOOK *moves in on* BISCUIT.)

**SPOOK.** I'm a bitch, now?

**BISCUIT.** Ain't what I'm sayin'.

**SPOOK.** Bullshit. All this talk about how "you're there for me" and "Bro," all that shit...

**BISCUIT.** Ain't like that.

**SPOOK.** Fuck that. Know, I never say "no" to nobody... 'cluding you. An' you know what I'm talkin' about!

**BISCUIT.** Motherfucker –

(BISCUIT *starts to rise,* SPOOK *pushes him back in his seat.*)

**ANDY.** *(to* SPOOK*)* Hey!

**SPOOK.** Think I want to come ask you for a job baggin' bodies? Hat in hand? How you think I feel?

**BISCUIT.** Listen here! If I could help I honest to shit would and you know that! (SPOOK *crosses away. beat)* C'mon, man. Look at me. No,no,no man. Don't be lookin' away. Look at me. *(He does so.)* If I could help, I would. Brother, I just can't. I can't.

(SPOOK *crosses back to the chairs and sits.* SPOOK *notices* ANDY *and* BILL *watching him. They look away. Pause.)*

**SPOOK.** 'Member seein' a kid swinging on this swing in Breyer Park, thinkin'...without our screws that thing'd fall apart. I made that. I *made* that. *I* did. So when people'd ask me where I was? " Elias Metal." Smilin' like a dumbass. So proud. Gave them my life.

(BISCUIT*'s pager goes off.)*

**BISCUIT.** Oh, man. *(beat)* We okay?

**SPOOK.** Yeah.

(BISCUIT *exits.* ARTIE, *still framed by the doorway opening, calls out.)*

**ARTIE.** Billy fuckin' Sims. Want you on the team, Waite.

**SPOOK.** Thanks!

**ARTIE.** Building a big moat in front of my castle, buddy. Which side you goin' be on?

(**ARTIE** *exits.*)

**BILL.** So, anyway…

**ANDY.** 6-8-7?

**BILL.** 5-8-7.

**ANDY.** Oh, I thought you said 6-8-7. What you play?

**BILL.** Oh, same. My 3-2-1. When it hits? Never work again.

**SPOOK.** …what they pay you there?

**BILL.** Oh, depends…on delivery, y'know? Eight seventy five an hour plus a dollar for every delivery I make. If it's heavy, like a battery an' 'at? Two bucks each.

**ANDY.** Play it in a box, or straight?

**BILL.** Straight.

**ANDY.** Play it in a box, have a better chance of hittin'.

**BILL.** Guess.

**SPOOK.** What about when you ain't drivin'?

**BILL.** Huh?

**SPOOK.** Over there. When you ain't making deliveries an' 'at?

**BILL.** Help out. Sweepin' an' stuff. Cleanin' up. But like today, we had nothin' goin' out, so they sent me home.

**SPOOK.** Paid?

**BILL.** Oh, no. If I don't work…you know –

**SPOOK.** Bunch of shit.

**BILL.** Oh, I don't mind. Least I got a job.

(**SPOOK** *crosses up to the bar.*)

**SPOOK.** Whaddya mean by that?

**BILL.** What?

**SPOOK.** That "Least you got a job." What's that mean?

**BILL.** Nothin'. Just –

(**SPOOK** *moves in on* **BILL.**)

**SPOOK.** 'Cause I'll get a job! Don't you worry, boy!

**BILL.** I didn't. I meant –

**SPOOK.** I'll find a job –

**ANDY.** – hey, hey, hey! Spook! I don't think he meant anything by it. I think he's just sayin'…all things considered, he's got a place to work!

**BILL.** Sure. I need the supplemental income. That's all.

**SPOOK.** I thought he was sayin'..

**ANDY.** See? Told you. Spook, gotta settle down.

**SPOOK.** …ahhh, I don't know what I thought.

(**SPOOK** *walks away.*)

**ANDY.** Sure.

(*Silence. The room settles.* **BILL** *starts rubbing his leg again.*)

**BILL.** Like jaggerbushes all up and down. Ever get that?

**ANDY.** Can't say I have.

**BILL.** Comes an' goes. Been comin' more than goin' lately.

**ANDY.** See a doc?

**BILL.** Maybe, huh? Least make some money.

**ANDY.** Don't make sense, they pay you to go to the hospital?

**BILL.** Only if I stay. Gotta stay. Then a hundred bucks a day.

**ANDY.** Huh.

**BILL.** 'Cause of the AARP, is why. Oh, it's the best.

**ANDY.** Your insurance?

**BILL.** I got Sarge's coverage for the stay. AARP just gives me money for the time inna hospital. All I gotta do is call Roberta with the days I was in, file a claim, couple months later get paid.

**ANDY.** Huh.

**BILL.** But I gotta pay 'em twenty four bucks a month.

**ANDY.** Oh.

**BILL.** But with the diabetes I got, an' heart problem, respiratory stuff…

**SPOOK.** (*grabbing the remote*) Gotta be a game on.

ANDY. *(to* BILL*)* Yeah, guess that AARP comes in handy.

SPOOK. Wings, Pistons...somethin'...

BILL. Worth it 'cause I got all of this stuff wrong with me. Somebody like you –

SPOOK. Guess they ain't.

ANDY. Shut it off.

SPOOK. I'll find somethin'. Somethin' gotta be on.

(BILL *goes back to his circular.*)

BILL. Hey, Kroger's got eggs on sale. One-twenty-nine a dozen.

ANDY. No kiddin'?

BILL. Huh. One per person. *(beat)* But if you go out, and come back in again? I keep a hat in my car. Put the hat on, go back in, get a second dozen one-twenty-nine.

ANDY. That work?

BILL. No. Well, they all know it's me, but I figure I put a hat on...I put a hat on, then the checker don't get in trouble if they're watchin' her. Don't want them losin' their job over a dozen eggs for one twenty nine.

ANDY. One-two-nine. You should play that.

BILL. Yeah. Oh, but don't tell Curtis. He don't know I shop there, but the prices are so good.

(SPOOK *shuts the tv off and sits at the bar*)

SPOOK. Can't believe there's no fuckin' game on!

BILL. Like jaggerbushes all up and down.

(BILL *begins to shake out his legs in a very broad manner.* ANDY *laughs.*)

SPOOK. Quit it, will ya?

(BILL *ignores him.*)

ANDY. *(laughing)* What the fuck you doin'?

BILL. Makes it feel better.

SPOOK. I said stop it.

(*He shakes his legs harder and harder.*)

ANDY. Watch where you're pointin' that can of yours, you could hurt somebody!

(**BILL** *playfully grinds like a stripper.*)

**BILL.** You wanna dance?

(**ANDY** *laughs harder, and starts to hum stripper music, prodding him on.*)

**SPOOK.** Said stop it…what the fuck, ya dumb assed fuck! Stop it!

(**SPOOK** *grabs* **BILL**, *and throws him against the wall.* **BILL** *falls to the ground.* **ANDY** *jumps in, breaking it up.*)

**ANDY.** Spook! Hey! Jesus Christ!

**SPOOK.** Ohhh, shit. Shit. Shit. I'm sorry, man. I'm –

**ANDY.** Here, Bill.

(**ANDY** *assists* **BILL** *to his stool.*)

**SPOOK.** Really, I'm –

**BILL.** – it's okay. It's okay.

**SPOOK.** Sorry –

**BILL.** No, no, you asked me to stop. It's just my leg hurt so much…ah…maybe I'll take a piss…

(**BILL** *heads off.*)

**ANDY.** What's goin' on?

**SPOOK.** Nothin'.

**ANDY.** Nothin'? Why take "nothin'" out on Housepie!?

**SPOOK.** I –

**ANDY.** Christ's sake. Guys come here to relax!

**SPOOK.** You're right.

**ANDY.** Goddamn right, I'm right! Now settle down! Shit!

(**SPOOK** *finishes his beer, pushes his empty glass towards* **ANDY**.)

**ANDY.** Nah, I'm makin' a call here. You're done for the night.

**SPOOK.** C'mon!

(**ANDY** *takes the empty glass, waves him off.*)

(**BILL** *returns, sits on his stool facing upstage. Silence.* **SPOOK** *pushes the pretzel bowl towards* **BILL**.)

**BILL.** *(to* **ANDY***)* I mix beer an' aspirins?

**ANDY.** Sure.

    *(silence)*

**BILL.** *(to* **SPOOK***)* Think I'll get sick mixin' beer an' aspirin?

**SPOOK.** No, you'll be alright. I do it alla time.

**BILL.** Andy?

    **(ANDY** *reaches underneath, grabs a bottle of aspirin and hands it over.)*

**BILL.** …ain't worth a nickle.

    *(Lights shift back to the pizza shop basement. We hear a recorded conversation between* **SPOOK** *and* **LARRY**.*)*

### Pizza Shop Basement – Thanksgiving Day

*(LIONS (6-5))*

*(As the conversation continues,* **SPOOK** *goes to his cot downstage right. On the wall above it hangs the dress shirt and tie Beth handed him in Act One. Taking off his Lions shirt, he puts on the dress shirt and tie.)*

**LARRY.** *(V.O.)* So, tomorrow. I don't want you to spend the holiday in the basement. Why don't you come over for Thanksgiving dinner with the family?

**SPOOK.** *(V.O.)* No, thanks...thanks, but I'm goin' over to... Katie's, I think.

**LARRY.** *(V.O.)* Oh...okay. But in case something changes –

**SPOOK.** *(V.O.)* But thanks...

**LARRY.** *(V.O.)* Sure. Wanna stop by for a beer, watch the game.

**SPOOK.** *(V.O.)* Okay. I'll think about it.

**LARRY.** *(V.O.)* Don't need to call or nothin', just stop by...

**SPOOK.** *(V.O.)* Okay.

**LARRY.** *(V.O.)* Anytime after one.

**SPOOK.** *(V.O.)* Okay. Like I said, probably be at Katie's, but I'll think about it.

*(He sits. Searching under the blanket, he finds a bottle of vodka in a brown paper bag. Takes a couple of swigs. Underneath this action, we hear the following.)*

**ANNOUNCER.** *(V.O.)* "...and it's so long from Ford Field in Detroit, where Brett Favre and the ten and one Green Bay Packers have defeated the six and five Detroit Lions. On behalf of myself and my partner hall of famer Willie Anderson, we wish you and yours a very, very happy Thanksgiving day!"

*(He pulls out a tattered business card. Looks at it. From the shadows,* **ARTIE** *enters and stands in a pool of light directly behind* **SPOOK**.*)*

*(***SPOOK** *stares straight out, never making eye contact with* **ARTIE**.*)*

**ARTIE.** So, John. Whaddya say? We celebratin'?

**SPOOK.** About that…

**ARTIE.** Yeah?

**SPOOK.** I been thinkin'. I just got promoted and Beth an' me –

**ARTIE.** What?

**SPOOK.** I just think, right now –

**ARTIE.** Is it the money? Fuck, man. I'm not bullshittin' you. I'm not makin' dick, either. Not now, but someday…

**SPOOK.** See, Artie. I don't know. You can live that kind of life. Me? I'm just a guy wants to work at Elias, raise my family, have a backyard…all I ever wanted.

**ARTIE.** This is the shit we dreamed about. Those rich fuckers lookin' down on us.

**SPOOK.** I know –

**ARTIE.** Billy Sims! Matt Millen.

**SPOOK.** I know. I know. I know.

**ARTIE.** Don't pass this up. Trust me. Do not pass this up.

**SPOOK.** Sorry. Thought long and hard about this.

**ARTIE.** What's Beth say?

**SPOOK.** Says it's up to me.

**ARTIE.** Well…?

**SPOOK.** I like it here.

**ARTIE.** You're sure?

**SPOOK.** I think it what's best.

**ARTIE.** Is it?

**SPOOK.** I think so.

**ARTIE.** I don't. I know *you*. An' I know *them*. You got an eye for…how many fucks you know, know Willie Anderson? None. None. None of those pinheaded, self important, silver spoon business son of bitches know sports. An' they especially didn't know him once he screwed up his knee. But we do, John. We know people. Poor fucks like Willie Anderson will just get railroaded by those business pricks every day of the goddamn week. But us, we'll treat the Willie Anderson's of the world with respect. And make a shitload of money because of it.

**SPOOK.** Artie –

**ARTIE.** I won't lie. I need ya, buddy. Need your help out there.

**SPOOK.** Yeah?

**ARTIE.** Yes! This is a chance of a lifetime…for both of us.

**SPOOK.** Don't know –

**ARTIE.** I do. Business world is cold. *(beat)* We'd go over Perino's, Feeg always says you can only trust your family behind the register? Never understood that. Now I do.

**SPOOK.** Jeez.

**ARTIE.** And you're family, John –

**SPOOK.** I can't.

**ARTIE.** You can't?

**SPOOK.** This just don't feel right. I can't.

**ARTIE.** No, no, no. Don't do this. Don't pass this up. John, someday you will look back on this chance. Tellin' you.

**SPOOK.** No. I won't.

**ARTIE.** No?

**SPOOK.** Not what I want, Artie. You're in New York, an' you like that. Me? Just want my house. Backyard. Wife. Kids. 'Sides, I got a great thing at Elias –

**ARTIE.** John! You gotta stop thinkin' like a fuckin' hillrat! I got a chance to leave here, took it and glad I did. This is *your* chance. Don't fuck it up –

**SPOOK.** Think wearin' that suit's gone to your head or somethin'. You hear me? I'm happy here. Ever think of that? I'm happy! You don't get that, then fuck off, alright?

*(silence)*

**SPOOK.** Sorry, Artie. I didn't mean it.

**ARTIE.** Sure you did. That's okay. One good thing about this business? Learn not to take shit personal.

**SPOOK.** Sorry.

**ARTIE.** Don't be. It's what you want.

**SPOOK.** I do.

**ARTIE.** Alright then.

**SPOOK.** But good luck with it, okay?

**ARTIE.** If you ever wanna see the big city.

**SPOOK.** Man! Your own card!

**ARTIE.** Just the start. Someday, I'll be wipin' my ass with "fuck you money."

(*ARTIE exits.* **SPOOK** *is left alone. We hear the following audio.*)

**BETH.** (*V.O.*) Hey, John. It's me. Look, don't know if you're still using this number. But if you are, and get this in time, the Placement Center called to confirm your appointment tomorrow. So...so...call them. Okay? So...oh...the number is 313-887-8500. Hope you get this. Bye.

(*Lights shift to.*)

### Career Placement Center – November 26 – Morning

**SPOOK.** …ate too much, 'course…but you know…

**MABEL.** Uh huh.

**SPOOK.** Family an' 'at…

**MABEL.** Right. Now the last time –

**SPOOK.** Yeah. Ate too much. We had…uh, whatchamacallit? Shit. *(beat)* Excuse me. You know…ummm…turkey.

**MABEL.** Well, it was Thanksgiving.

**SPOOK.** Yeah, Thanksgiving. Giving for thanks.

*(silence)*

**MABEL.** Yes, well. Lets take a look at what we have for you.

**SPOOK.** Lemme guess. Service jobs. Got them service jobs, right?

**MABEL.** We also have a delivery job.

**SPOOK.** Drivin' stuff around?

**MABEL.** Exactly.

**SPOOK.** Gimme somethin' good to drive?

**MABEL.** Sorry?

**SPOOK.** Would it be a good car?

**MABEL.** You'd have to supply your own vehicle.

**SPOOK.** That's not gonna work.

**MABEL.** Why not?

**SPOOK.** No car.

**MABEL.** I thought you said you had a car?

**SPOOK.** Got rid of it. 'Cause, honest, most stuff is right here. After insurance and tryin' to get a parking spot and gettin' ripped off. I don't need a car. If I wanted a car, that's one thing, okay?

**MABEL.** I understand. Let's move on…

**SPOOK.** 'Cause I don't need one. I had one and…never used it. Piece of shit anyway.

**MABEL.** Mr. Waite. It's nine twenty five in the morning.

**SPOOK.** Uh huh.

**MABEL.** Drinking before a job interview is unacceptable behavior.

**SPOOK.** Drinkin'? I ain't been –

**MABEL.** – unacceptable!

**SPOOK.** I ain't!

**MABEL.** You haven't been drinking?

**SPOOK.** No.

**MABEL.** And you're telling me the truth?

**SPOOK.** I…I haven't.

**MABEL.** Do I look like a fool, Mr. Waite? I can smell it from here, on your breath.

**SPOOK.** I told you –

**MABEL.** I'll give you one more chance. Are you saying you haven't been drinking? That's what you're telling me?

*(Silence. She stares at him.)*

**MABEL.** I can be your ally or your enemy. What's it going to be? *(silence)* Well?

*(She gets up to leave.)*

**SPOOK.** I uh, yeah. I…I got so nervous last time and I thought…take the edge off. For nerves. It won't happen again. Honest.

**MABEL.** Well, since we're being honest. Let me be frank. The only reason you're still here is because of Reverend Stuyvants.

**SPOOK.** He's a good guy.

**MABEL.** Yes, he is. But Mr. Waite, we will not get anywhere if you continue this type of behavior.

**SPOOK.** It's not a regular thing. Honest.

**MABEL.** Honest?

**SPOOK.** You gotta give me another…*(beat)* I need to do good here. I need to – *(beat)* Yeah, I had a couple shots before I got here today, but you gotta believe me. It was just to…just to…I mean, I'm wearin' a tie an' everything. I'm showin' respect.

**MABEL.** *(beat)* Go home and sleep it off. Come back here one week from today. Same time, okay?

**SPOOK.** Okay.

**MABEL.** And next time? Sober.

*(He exits. Lights fade.)*

## 10th Ward Club – December 16 – Evening

*(LIONS (6-8))*

*(In the darkness we hear the following audio as the lights rise.)*

*(**BILL, CURTIS, GAIL** and **LARRY** are hanging out. **LENNIE** is behind the bar.)*

**TV ANNOUNCER.** *(V.O.)* …Tomlinson showed why he's the league M.V.P. Rushes for over a hundred yards and scores two touchdowns. Stu, Chargers flat out dominated the Lions, 51-14. Now? Norv Turner's club is in first place. And the Lions? Back where they always are. At or near the bottom of the N.F.C North, a pathetic six and eight.

*(**LARRY**, remote in hand, shuts TV off.)*

**LARRY.** Fuck you, Schlereth.

**BILL.** I'll give you twenty bucks for gas…

**CURTIS.** …sure. What time?

**BILL.** Flight leaves at eight forty five, so…Seven? That too early?

**CURTIS.** No, I'll pick you up quarter till.

**BILL.** Thanks.

**CURTIS.** No problem. Off tomorrow, so…

*(**ANDY** enters wearing a Santa Claus hat and a holiday sweater. Pulls out a paper from his backpack.)*

**ANDY.** Ho, ho, ho! Got an early Christmas present from the North Pole! Drumroll, Lennie.

*(**LENNIE** pounds the bar.)*

**ANDY.** Check it out, "A-plus!" Business math final! One more math class and I'm done!

*(Congratulations all around.)*

**LENNIE.** Lemme see that!

*(**ANDY** crosses behind the bar.)*

*(buzzer)*

**LENNIE.** 10th Ward.

**SPOOK.** *(O.S.)* Spook.

(**SPOOK** *enters.*)

**LARRY.** Spook.

**SPOOK.** Hey.

**LARRY.** How you doin'?

**SPOOK.** You know.

(*He takes off his jacket to reveal a "CVS CAREMARK" shirt. He wears a name tag that reads, "Hello. My name is John."*)

**LARRY.** Catch any of it?

**SPOOK.** Like that much. Close up the shop already?

**LARRY.** Fuck yeah. Since they started to losin' again…

**SPOOK.** See Biscuit?

**CURTIS.** Left at the half.

**SPOOK.** Look what I got.

(*holds up a compact disc*)

**SPOOK.** Those songs him and Shawn did? Got 'em off the internet.

**GAIL.** You went on the internet?

**SPOOK.** No. Kid at work did it for me. That "MySpace" thing. *(to* **ANDY***)* We put it on?

**ANDY.** Why?

**SPOOK.** Hear it.

**ANDY.** Right.

**SPOOK.** No, really.

**GAIL.** Any good?

**SPOOK.** Who cares? It's Biscuit an' Shawn! *(off* **ANDY***'s look)* What?

**ANDY.** Nothin'.

(**ANDY** *goes to get his school bag. As he crosses back toward the bar,* **SPOOK** *grabs his arm,* **ANDY** *shakes him off.*)

**SPOOK.** No. You were like…with this face.

**ANDY.** Just wonder where he's goin' with it.

**SPOOK.** Who knows?

(**ANDY** *crosses back behind the bar.*)

**ANDY.** Oh, yeah. I'm sure there's a record contract just waitin' for him and his gangster nephew.

**SPOOK.** Least he's tryin'.

**BILL.** Yeah, all you need is that one song. Like on "American Idol." That Clay Aiken. He was nothin', now he's rich.

**ANDY.** Biscuit? Oh, come on! Nice enough guy, but look at him. See these guys on TV, they're half his age.

**SPOOK.** Fuck you.

**LARRY.** John.

**SPOOK.** Nah, sick of this shit. He sits back there all the time passin' judgment. Who are you to piss on this guy's dreams?

**ANDY.** I'm not.

**SPOOK.** You are.

(**ANDY** *dismisses him and turns his back.*)

**SPOOK.** Don't blow me off. I ain't some jackoff pinhead from your school.

(**SPOOK** *tries to go behind the bar.* **LENNIE** *stops him.*)

**LENNIE.** Hey!

**ANDY.** I wasn't –

**SPOOK.** Dimes to donuts, if Biscuit was here, you wouldn't say this shit. You'd smile, put the CD on.

**ANDY.** Bullshit. I speak my mind.

**SPOOK.** So hard to say, "Good for him"? Or say nothin' at all? Here's a newsflash,….YOU'RE A GUY FROM THE NEIGHBORHOOD! Ain't no better than any other hillrat in this club!

**ANDY.** Settle down!

**SPOOK.** Fuck you, settle down! Sick of your shit!

(**SPOOK** *tosses a beer in* **ANDY**'s *face, then lunges at him. The men pull him away before he can get over the bar. The place erupts. The following is almost completely overlapped.*)

**LARRY.** Whoa!!! Whoa!!! Jesus Christ!

**LENNIE.** Hey!

**GAIL.** Settle down.

**SPOOK.** Fuck that. *(to* **ANDY***)* C'mon, man! Let's go.

**LARRY.** Stop it.

**ANDY.** That's it! I'm done here! Not goin' take this anymore! Had it up to here puttin' up with ignorant
drunk bastards like him!

**SPOOK.** Fuck you!

**ANDY.** You can deal with his shit. Not me. I'm gone.

(**ANDY** *grabs his bag and jacket, throws his keys down.
Starts off.*)

**LENNIE.** What?

**ANDY.** I quit!

**LENNIE.** The hell you do.

**SPOOK.** That's right. Go. Go ahead and quit.

**LARRY.** Guys. What the –

**ANDY.** I'm gone. Asshole's all yours, Len!

(*He leaves.* **BILL** *runs after him.*)

(**SPOOK** *stands clapping.*)

**SPOOK.** See? Says it as he's leavin', don't have the balls to
stick around and say it to my face like a man.

**LENNIE.** Thanks a fuckin' lot, Spook. Been here all goddamn day, now I gotta close too!

**SPOOK.** Andy's fault. Better off anyway.

**LENNIE.** *(seeing the mess on the bar)* And I ain't cleanin' this
up, either. You fuckin' clean it up!

**SPOOK.** Fine.

(**LENNIE** *exits. As the dust clears* **CURTIS**, **GAIL** *and*
**LARRY** *stare at* **SPOOK***.*)

**LARRY.** What the fuck?

**SPOOK.** He's an asshole, Lar.

(**LARRY** *takes* **SPOOK** *in.*)

**SPOOK.** What you think I'm in the wrong?

**LARRY.** Not sayin' shit.

**SPOOK.** Got somethin' on your mind say it.

**LARRY.** What am I gonna say? How can you pull that shit here in the club? You do that, you end up looking like…

**SPOOK.** What? Like what?

**LARRY.** This is our club. Our *club*!

**SPOOK.** I know where I'm at. What I wanna know is how it makes me look?

**LARRY.** (How the) hell should I know?

**SPOOK.** How, Larry? How? Don't start some shit, you ain't ready to finish.

**LARRY.** Forget it. Look fine.

**SPOOK.** I look fine? What the fuck is that? You just got done sayin' – Jesus. My own friend gonna bullshit me?

**LARRY.** C'mon –

**SPOOK.** How 'bout you guys? Gonna bullshit me, too? Curtis?

**CURTIS.** Nah.

(**CURTIS** *exits.*)

**SPOOK.** How about you, Gail? You gonna bullshit me?

**GAIL.** No. You look tired, rundown and drunk. Again.

**SPOOK.** Oh, yeah?

**GAIL.** Yeah. And I'm too old for this high school shit. Grow up.

(*She leaves.*)

**SPOOK.** See that? That's a friend for ya. I want lies, I'll call Andy back here. Any more lies for me, Larry?

**LARRY.** You're out of line, buddy –

**SPOOK.** Buddy? Buddy!? Fuck you. Think 'cause you let me stay in your cellar you can talk down to me?

**LARRY.** Talk *down* to you? Talk *down* to you? Who the fuck are *you*? Who made you king of the club? Nobody, that's who, 'cause you ain't. I ain't gonna take that personal 'cause I know you're fucked up an' ain't been right for awhile now. But as bad as shit may be, don't insinuate I ain't a friend. Known you 'fore you had fuzz on your nuts. How far we go back? Never said no to you for nothin'. Ever. Hold your checks, never charge ya for a sandwich…I'm even gonna forget the way you're lookin' at me right now 'cause I'm a friend. Don't ever say I ain't. And don't talk to me like I'm some fuckin' hillrat.

SPOOK. Puttin' words in my mouth.

LARRY. You can't take shit out on people at will. Fight the world all you want, John. You'll wear out 'fore it does.

(*LARRY exits. SPOOK sits, alone. After a moment, he gets up to begin cleaning the place up.*)

(*BISCUIT enters.*)

SPOOK. Just the motherfucker I'm lookin' for. *(No response)* Wait. Just wait. Wait 'till you hear what I got. Biscuit? Check it out.

(*SPOOK places the CD in the player. It begins to play. BISCUIT recognizes it as his music.*)

BISCUIT. Shut it off, please.

SPOOK. C'mon…

BISCUIT. Shut that thing off.

SPOOK. You and Shawn. From the internet. Didn't think I could find –

BISCUIT. Please. Can I get my music?

SPOOK. C'mon, it's –

BISCUIT. Can I get my goddamn music?

(*SPOOK shuts the music off, takes the CD from the player, hands it over.*)

SPOOK. Take it, then.

BISCUIT. Thank you.

(*BISCUIT takes the CD. Stares at it. After a moment, he goes behind the bar and grabs a bottle of whiskey, crosses downstage. Sits.*)

SPOOK. What's goin' on?

**BISCUIT.** Nothin'.

**SPOOK.** Don't seem like nothin' to me.

**BISCUIT.** Yeah, well.

*(silence)*

**SPOOK.** See the game?

*(no response)*

**SPOOK.** Didn't miss much, or so I hear. Had to work, too. So…

**BISCUIT.** Got my fourteen dollars. All that matters, right? Fourteen goddamn dollars.

*(silence)*

**BISCUIT.** Know what I made in '06 'fore taxes an' shit? Nineteen thousand dollars. Talkin' the whole year.

**SPOOK.** Man…

**BISCUIT.** …but today I'm one rich motherfucker. City give me fourteen whole dollars for baggin' my nephew.

**SPOOK.** *(sotto)* What?

**BISCUIT.** Got that page. Says "5502 Cass." I get there, see this body behind the dumpster. Put my gloves on, turn it over an' see Shawn. Dead. Layin' there dead behind dumpster. What's he doin' over Cass Corridor? Something shot him. Shot him and left him.

*(silence)*

Boy loved baseball. That his game, right? Took that boy to Tiger Stadium for his first game. Bought him one of them "Made in Taiwan" piece of shit balls with the stamped autographs they sell. Kept sayin', "Uncle Lee, this ball worth a million dollars. A million dollars!" *(beat)* Once he growed, walked past his room. See he still kept it. Ask him why, he say, "Cause it worth a million dollars." I said, "Boy you crazy." "Uncle Lee, it worth a million dollars 'cause you give it to me." There I am in that alley and all I see is that little kid. Almost couldn't do it. I mean, put my Shawn in a bag? Then I thought, least it be me baggin' him. *(long pause)* Been baggin' folks so long I forgot they be somebody's

husband, somebody's brother, somebody's son. Somebody's baby. *(beat)* Goddamn! I never wanted to do this,
man. Never. You got to be a cold, cold motherfucker to
do this here job. Just needed to feed my kids.

*(silence)*

**BISCUIT.** He dead. Shawn dead. Ain't I a rich man?

*(Lights fade down.)*

## 10th Ward Club – December 30

*(LIONS (7-9))*

*(In the darkness, we hear audio.)*

*(**LENNIE** is behind the bar, pouring a beer. **REV** and **BILL** are getting ready to leave. **SPOOK** sits silently, looking straight out.)*

*(From the TV, audio of the Local sports wrap-up show is heard. The audio should play underneath the men's exit.)*

**TV ANNOUNCER.** *(V.O.)* ...Brett Favre goes nine of eleven for ninety nine yards and two touchdowns in what was his two hundred and fifty third consecutive start. As for our Lions...a different story. We started six and two, then end up going one and seven to end at seven and nine.

**TV ANNOUNCER #2.** *(V.O.)* – Yeah, seven and nine.

**TV ANNOUNCER.** *(V.O.)* Yeah...and you finish like that. Somebody, you know, has to take the fall. I think, and this is just me, but I think the most likely scapegoat will be Mike Martz. I'm betting the mad scientist will be looking for a new offense to tinker with next season.

*(**REV** gets up to leave.)*

**REV.** Lennie. John, see you fellas tomorrow.

**BILL.** Rev...

*(**REV** leaves.)*

**TV ANNOUNCER #2.** *(V.O.)* -But this goes beyond Martz. 'Cause we all know that Marinelli is a defense first type of a coach. He likes the three fingers in the dirt kind of guys. Guys that are going to punish you when you touch the ball. Martz, well, you know, he comes with a label. He likes that spread offense that worked in St. Louis when he had weapons like Holt and Warner.

**TV ANNOUNCER.** *(V.O.)* Greatest show on turf-

**TV ANNOUNCER #2.** *(V.O.)* Yeah. Exactly. The Lions don't have those tools. If I'm the Lions organization, I'm looking at all areas. Offense, defense, special teams. Find out where this thing went bad.

*(**BILL** starts to leave.)*

**BILL.** Yeah. Me, too. 'Night, John. Lennie.

**LENNIE.** Housepie.

*(He leaves.)*

**TV ANNOUNCER #2.** *(V.O.)* And I'd put the guys on notice. Make them take a good look in the mirror and ask themselves if they want to be here. Be accountable for the collapse this season. Look, lets not kid ourselves, they need to get tougher up front, keep Kitna upright. Upgrade the return game-

**TV ANNOUNCER.** *(V.O.)* Free agency?

**TV ANNOUNCER #2.** *(V.O.)* Maybe. They have the cap space. But who's available, and more importantly, who wants to play here-

*(**LENNIE** brings the beer to **SPOOK**. Using the remote he shuts off the TV.)*

**LENNIE.** We make this one the last, Spook? Wanna get outta here on time for a change.

*(**LARRY** enters carrying a pizza.)*

**LENNIE.** I'm closin'.

**LARRY.** No, I know. Got stuck with this pie.

**LENNIE.** Okay, thanks.

*(**LENNIE** takes it. **LARRY** walks over to **SPOOK** and pats him on the back.)*

**LARRY.** See ya tomorrow?

*(**SPOOK** nods "yes.")*

*(Suddenly, offstage we hear **GAIL**'s loud voice. She is singing.)*

**GAIL.** "I got a feeling, Packers goin' to the Super Bowl!"

**LARRY.** 'night.

*(**GAIL** enters as **LARRY** exits.)*

**GAIL.** "I got a feeling Packers goin' to the Super Bowl!"

**LENNIE.** I'm tryin' to get outta here.

**GAIL.** *(She ignores him.)* "I got a feeling Packers goin' to the Super Bowl!"

**LENNIE.** Gail! I'm tryin' to get outta here!

(**LENNIE** *throws a towel at her. She catches it. Laughs.*)

**GAIL.** I'm not stayin'!

**SPOOK.** Just comin' in to gloat.

(**LENNIE** *takes the pizza and exits.*)

**GAIL.** Nope. Just came to tell ya how sweet it's gonna be watchin' my Packers in the playoffs this year. Coulda been the Lions…the cryin' Lions, but they couldn't win when it counted, so they're stayin' home an' we're movin' on!

**SPOOK.** Why couldn't they just show up? Show a little pride? If we'd of won today you'd be singing a different tune. We'd of won today…and got a little help…we might of got a wild card and made the playoffs. The playoffs! Woulda been the lead story on ESPN, coulda been on the cover of USA TODAY –

**GAIL.** Coulda, woulda, shoulda. And if my Aunt Frances had balls, she'd be my Uncle Frank.

**SPOOK.** Fuck you.

**GAIL.** Huh?

**SPOOK.** Said, "Fuck you." What are you, deaf?

**GAIL.** A little. See, it's tough hearing you with all these championship rings in my ears.

(**SPOOK** *sits in silence.*)

**GAIL.** Hey, c'mon…I'm just havin' a little fun here.

**SPOOK.** This was the year. I know I say that every year, but this year? I really needed this year to be the year.

**GAIL.** Did look good for awhile.

**SPOOK.** Sometimes, I get these…I don't know what you call 'em, "rememberences" or somethin'. Like I'm walkin' down the street an' the air smells like it used to back when we was all workin'. Been a tough year. The plant closin' an'…Tough year. (*beat*) Ah, you don't wanna hear this –

**GAIL.** It's okay.

**SPOOK.** Not anymore. Nothing's okay anymore.

(**SPOOK** *stares ahead.* **GAIL** *crosses to the chairs and sits.*)

**SPOOK.** Seen her?

**GAIL.** Yeah.

**SPOOK.** Yeah?

**GAIL.** Yeah.

**SPOOK.** And…?

**GAIL.** …good.

**SPOOK.** Talk to her?

**GAIL.** Sure.

**SPOOK.** Ever ask 'bout me?

**GAIL.** Couple times.

**SPOOK.** Did?

**GAIL.** Asked how you were. You know.

**SPOOK.** Fucked up with her. When I miss her most? Sayin' goodnight. Lyin' in bed. Holding her close. Feeling her breath on the back of my neck. Then, right before she'd go to sleep, she'd whisper in my ear, "Goodnight, honey. Love you." Real soft like. Miss that.

(*silence*)

**SPOOK.** What happened? I had this great life. Woke up one day and it was gone. Like I was in another country. We built this country. Without us, this country wouldn't be what it is. Then I think…what are we? Ain't got nothin' really. What we got? Service jobs?

**GAIL.** Gettin' pretty heavy here.

**SPOOK.** Sorry. I'll shut up.

**GAIL.** No, it's okay. Tryin' to add a little levity. Lift your mood. (*beat*) "Colorado Bob."

(*They share a laugh.*)

**GAIL.** I remember for the longest time thinking my life would change when the Pack won in '96. Next day, still had to go to work. Still broke. Still alone. Saw their victory parade and it dawned on me…that's their life, not mine. *(beat)* I will admit, though, that on that day when people looked at me, I felt like they were smilin' at me insteada laughin'.

**SPOOK.** Think people laugh at ya?

**GAIL.** Sometimes.

**SPOOK.** Really?

**GAIL.** Don't *you?* Behind my back?

**SPOOK.** Kiddin'? Everybody likes Gail Finch.

**GAIL.** C'mon, I'm bein' honest with you here, an' you're fuckin' with me.

**SPOOK.** Wouldn't fuck with you if we didn't like you. You know how it works. The more we fuck with ya, the more we like ya. *(beat)* Everybody loves Gail Finch.

**GAIL.** Serious?

**SPOOK.** As a heart attack.

**GAIL.** Good to know.

*(awkward silence)*

**GAIL.** Well, uh…better go. Gotta open tomorrow. Irene's got that cataract surgery, so…

**SPOOK.** …real early then.

*(She starts to leave, turns back.)*

**GAIL.** Here I thought I was doin' such a great job of bein' a pain in the ass!

*(She leaves.)*

*(**SPOOK** stares at his beer, for a long time. Then takes it to the bar, pours it down the sink and exits.)*

*(lights fade)*

### The 10th Ward Club – February, 2008

*(The day after the Super Bowl.)*

*(As the lights rise, we see **CURTIS** sitting at the bar. **BILL** and **LENNIE** shoot pool.)*

*(A talk show, such as the Jerry Springer Show or something similar, plays in the background.)*

**BILL.** How many you play?

**LENNIE.** Bought five squares. Most of my numbers were shit, but I hit that fuckin' first quarter. Still can't believe New England lost that game.

**CURTIS.** Told Gail, if I was a gambler I'd of bet on the Giants.

**LENNIE.** Should've.

**CURTIS.** Said *if* I did. I don't. I'm just sayin'. I knew they'd win.

**LENNIE.** Yeah.

**CURTIS.** Still. Best Super Bowl in a long time, huh?

**LENNIE.** Not bad.

*(pause, as they continue to play)*

**BILL.** Gettin' cold out there.

**LENNIE.** Yep.

**BILL.** Supposed to get down to three degrees tonight. Could be worse. Hear on the TV, Boulder is gettin' two feet of snow tomorrow.

**LENNIE.** Sucks for Colorado Bob.

**BILL.** Who?

**LENNIE.** Your girl. Colorado Bob.

**BILL.** What are you talkin' about?

**LENNIE.** That girl you got out in Colorado.

**BILL.** How you know about her?

**LENNIE.** How I know? Everybody knows. Thought you knew, we knew.

**BILL.** No.

**LENNIE.** Andy was tellin' us what she looked like an' 'at. It's okay. Gettin' a little taste? Good for you.

**BILL.** *(beat)* Roberta. Her name's Roberta.

**LENNIE.** Larry made it up, not me.

**BILL.** Larry?

**LENNIE.** Yeah. And from what Andy says? Stick with Bob.

**BILL.** Fuck you!

(**BILL** *throws the stick down and crosses to the bar, sits facing upstage.*)

**LENNIE.** Hey, what's the matter? *(beat)* You should hear the shit your friend Andy usta say. Really nasty stuff.

**BILL.** Why would he do that?

**LENNIE.** Fuckin' around. Why we do anything?

**BILL.** You know she said to tell him "hi"? Wanted to meet him someday.

**LENNIE.** Ain't gotta worry about that no more.

*(silence)*

**BILL.** Can't believe him.

(**LENNIE** *puts away the pool sticks, crosses behind the bar, addresses* **BILL.**)

**LENNIE.** Knew you were fuckin' her, didn't know you really liked her. Sorry.

(**BILL** *moves away from the bar, sits downstage.*)

*(silence)*

(**LENNIE** *takes the remote, mutes the TV.*)

(**CURTIS** *approaches* **BILL** *cautiously. He stands near him, not knowing what to say.* **BILL** *finally notices him.*)

**CURTIS.** She nice, Bill?

*(pause)*

**BILL.** Curtis, she's…oh, boy!

**CURTIS.** That's good.

**BILL.** I know she ain't a model or nothin', but so? She cares about me. An' who am I? Nobody, that's who. But when I'm with her, or talkin' to her on the phone, I wanna…I don't know. Know how long it's been since I felt that way?

CURTIS. No.

BILL. I've never felt that way. Never.

CURTIS. But you're married.

BILL. Yeah, but I never loved her.

CURTIS. C'mon…

BILL. No.

CURTIS. But why would you stay married-?

BILL. What you did back then. Stuck it out. Lots of times, I think if I was born thirty some years later, I might of had a real life.

*(beat)*

CURTIS. But now you got Roberta.

(**BILL** *smiles, crosses back up to the bar.*)

BILL. They show the number yet?

LENNIE. After Springer.

BILL. Got a good feeling today.

*(beat)*

CURTIS. They get snow in Tennessee?

BILL. I dunno.

CURTIS. That's down south, huh?

LENNIE. Then I don't think they do.

BILL. If my number hits today –

LENNIE. – maybe they do. I dunno. Why?

CURTIS. Considerin' my options.

LENNIE. What? To use your right or left hand when you're jackin' off?

CURTIS. Funny. Got an opportunity down there.

BILL. Sure that's the right one?

LENNIE. I know my channels. Couple more minutes.

CURTIS. Stepfather? Showed me this internet site where they post jobs. Like the Free Press only on the computer.

BILL. You got a computer?

CURTIS. Use his. An' they got these sites –

**LENNIE.** Yeah, like that Monster-dot-com an' that shit. I seen them commercials on the TV.

**CURTIS.** I don't know. Think it was somethin' else.

**LENNIE.** All the fuckin' same.

(**BILL** *takes the last pretzel from the bowl.*)

**LENNIE.** Jesus Christ! I just filled that fucker up!

**BILL.** Don't cost you nothin'!

**LENNIE.** Yeah, but I gotta fill it up again!

(**LENNIE** *takes the bowls away from* **BILL** *in a punitive manner and crosses from behind the bar.*)

**CURTIS.** I'm tired of baggin' them groceries over there. Know what though? When I told Garlow about Tennessee, he told me to hold off. He might have somethin' for me in produce!

**LENNIE.** Dumbass. Why did you tell him?

**CURTIS.** They wanted references from places I'd worked. Lampert's is the only place I ever been, so I had to ask for a letter to take with me.

**LENNIE.** He'll fuck ya. Watch.

**CURTIS.** Why?

**LENNIE.** Keep you there.

**CURTIS.** Nah, we're friends, too. He's not just my manager.

**LENNIE.** Mark my words, he's gonna fuck ya.

(**CURTIS** *crosses away from* **LENNIE** *to* **BILL.**)

**CURTIS.** This thing in Tennessee's different. It ain't a supermarket. It's for security. Twelve twenty-five an hour. All I gotta do is ride around in a car, an' see that nobody breaks into the houses.

**BILL.** They let ya listen to the radio?

**CURTIS.** Dunno.

**LENNIE.** Probably gotta a scanner in there, like they got on that "Cops."

**BILL.** I like listenin' to the radio when I'm drivin'.

**LENNIE.** Shit, yeah. You gotta have diversions. Like here onna TV? I got Walker the Texas Ranger, Jag, Andy from Mayberry, Sanford and Son, Stooges, Springer, the number, local news, Sportscenter, pre-game shit, then whatever games on.

**BILL.** Helps pass the day.

**LENNIE.** Is the day.

*(**SPOOK** enters. Hangs up his coat. He is in a dress shirt and tie. Goes behind the bar.)*

**SPOOK.** Hey sports fans.

**ALL.** Hey, Spook.

**SPOOK.** Cold out there.

*(**LENNIE** crosses up to the bar.)*

**LENNIE.** *(references the cash register)* Still gotta change the drawer over.

*(**SPOOK** nods. Pours himself a coffee.)*

**LENNIE.** How'd it go?

**SPOOK.** Good. Had a good time. Katie stopped by. That was nice. *(beat)* A start, y'know?

*(silence)*

**CURTIS.** Yeah. If Garlow gives me the produce section…

**BILL.** Where you goin' again?

**CURTIS.** Tennessee.

**BILL.** That's in Nashville. All them country singers live there.

**CURTIS.** Hear country girls are hot. Never been with a girl outside of here. Be somethin', fuck a girl talks southern!

**LENNIE.** That box ain't got no twang.

**CURTIS.** Still. I think I wanna find out. Tennessee. An' I won't have to bag no more. Just drive around and watch houses. An' they said there's growth potential, too.

**BILL.** Yeah?

**CURTIS.** Yeah! I get excited just thinkin' about it. But then I get worried thinkin' about leavin'. Not knowin' nobody over there an' 'at. Kinda scary. *(beat)* Spook, What you think?

**SPOOK.** Get out of here. Go to Tennessee, D.C, Wherever... just go. Hell, you've done this. Go do that. We'll still be here. *(beat. He toasts with his coffee)* Tennessee!

**LENNIE.** Hey, the number!

*(**LENNIE** grabs the remote.)*

*(The theme from the "Daily Number" plays. With the exception of **SPOOK**, all the men pull out their lottery tickets.)*

**ANNOUNCER.** Let's play the Michigan lottery! Live this evening Monday, February 4th, 2008. Thanks to today's witness David Bertram. And now, today's Daily Number. The first digit is...

*(The audio goes silent, and we never hear any of the winning numbers. All that remains are the men looking hopefully at the screen.)*

*(Slow fade to black.)*

**End of Play**

# GLOSSARY

BARRY SANDERS – Hall of fame running back drafted by the Lions in 1989 with the third overall pick in the first round. Considered by many experts to be one of the greatest players to ever to play the game.

BILLY SIMS – A running back taken with the first overall pick in the 1980 NFL Draft. He led the Lions to the playoffs in 1982 and 1983. A knee injury ended his career midway through the 1984 season. Sims remains a beloved former sports figure in Detroit.

FAVRE – Brett Favre. Green Bay Packer icon and starting quarterback from 1992 to 2007.

DRAFT DAY – The day NFL teams have an opportunity to select a player coming out of college.

ELWAY – John Elway. Denver Broncos hall of fame quarterback.

GRIESE – Brian Griese. Quarterback drafted by Denver to replace the retiring John Elway. Son of Hall of Fame quarterback Bob Griese.

JON KITNA – Lions starting quarterback from 2006 to 2008.

MATT MILLEN – General Manager of the Lions from 2000 to 2008.

N.F.L – The National Football League.

N.F.C North Division – The National Football League North division is comprised of the following teams: Chicago Bears, Detroit Lions, Green Bay Packers and the Minnesota Vikings.

"NUMBER ONE PICK" – Refers to the first player selected by a team in the draft.

SPYGATE – Scandal where the New England Patriots were caught illegally taping other teams practices and games.

Printed in the United States
144141LV00001B/1/P

9 780573 696312